Personal Best

B1 Pre-intermediate

Student's Book and Workbook combined edition **A**

Series Editor
Jim Scrivener

Student's Book Authors
Bess Bradfield with
Graham Fruen

Workbook Authors
Elizabeth Walter and
Kate Woodford

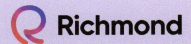

STUDENT'S BOOK CONTENTS

	LANGUAGE			SKILLS	
	GRAMMAR	PRONUNCIATION	VOCABULARY		
1 All about me 1A The only friends you need p4 1B 21st century hobbies p6 1C Famous families p8 1D Me in three objects p10	■ simple present and adverbs and expressions of frequency ■ present continuous and simple present	■ final -s/-es sound ■ -ng sound	■ personality adjectives ■ hobbies and socializing ■ useful verbs	**LISTENING** ■ a video about our hobbies and how we socialize ■ listening for the main idea ■ contractions	**WRITING** ■ making notes ■ expressing reasons and results (so, because, that's why) **PERSONAL BEST** ■ a blog post about personal objects
2 Stories and pictures 2A That's me in the photo! p12 2B Party like it's 1829 p14 2C Behind the camera p16 2D That reminds me of … p18	■ simple past and time expressions ■ question forms	■ -ed endings ■ question intonation	■ -ed/-ing adjectives ■ life stages	**READING** ■ a text about Andrew Jackson's parties at the White House ■ approaching a text ■ sequencers (after, later, then)	**SPEAKING** ■ showing interest ■ telling a personal story **PERSONAL BEST** ■ talking about a personal story
1 and 2 REVIEW and PRACTICE p20					
3 Keep on traveling 3A Tourist or traveler? p22 3B Staycation or vacation? p24 3C A traveler's tale p26 3D Travel problems p28	■ comparatives, superlatives, (not) as … as ■ past continuous and simple past	■ sentence stress ■ was/were	■ useful adjectives ■ vacation activities	**LISTENING** ■ a video about the popularity of staycations ■ identifying key points ■ sentence stress	**WRITING** ■ writing a narrative ■ adverbs of manner **PERSONAL BEST** ■ a story about a travel problem
4 The working world 4A The future of work p30 4B I'm so bored! p32 4C The secret boss p34 4D Can I leave a message? p36	■ will, may and might for predictions ■ be going to and present continuous for plans and arrangements	■ want/won't ■ going to and want to	■ jobs ■ phrases about work	**READING** ■ a text about how boredom can improve creativity ■ skimming a text ■ pronoun referencing	**SPEAKING** ■ dealing with difficulties ■ telephone language **PERSONAL BEST** ■ making arrangements by phone
3 and 4 REVIEW and PRACTICE p38					
5 Mind and body 5A Should I see a doctor? p40 5B Modern life is stressful p42 5C How to be happy p44 5D I need your advice p46	■ should/shouldn't (for advice and suggestions) ■ first conditional	■ should/shouldn't ■ 'll contraction	■ health and medicine ■ verb collocations (do, make, have and take) ■ emotions and feelings	**LISTENING** ■ a video about how we react to stress ■ listening in detail ■ linking consonants and vowels	**WRITING** ■ writing an informal e-mail ■ modifiers **PERSONAL BEST** ■ an informal e-mail to a friend asking for advice
6 Risks and experiences 6A Try something new! p48 6B An amazing story p50 6C Into the wild p52 6D Would you take the risk? p54	■ present perfect with ever and never ■ second conditional	■ irregular past participles ■ sentence stress	■ phrasal verbs ■ the natural world	**READING** ■ an article about Aron Ralston's survival story ■ guessing the meaning of words from context ■ linkers to add extra information (and, also, as well, and too)	**SPEAKING** ■ taking turns ■ agreeing and disagreeing **PERSONAL BEST** ■ having a group discussion
5 and 6 REVIEW and PRACTICE p56					

Grammar practice p112   Vocabulary practice p136   Communication practice p158   Irregular verbs p175

Language App, unit-by-unit grammar and vocabulary games

WORKBOOK CONTENTS

		LANGUAGE			SKILLS	
		GRAMMAR	PRONUNCIATION	VOCABULARY		
1 All about me **1A** p2 **1B** p3 **1C** p4 **1D** p5		▪ simple present and adverbs of frequency ▪ present continuous and simple present	▪ final -s/-es sound ▪ -ng sound	▪ personality adjectives ▪ hobbies and socializing ▪ useful verbs	LISTENING ▪ listening for the main idea	WRITING ▪ making notes
1 — REVIEW and PRACTICE		p6				
2 Stories and pictures **2A** p8 **2B** p9 **2C** p10 **2D** p11		▪ simple past and time expressions ▪ question forms	▪ -ed endings ▪ question intonation	▪ -ed/-ing adjectives ▪ life stages	READING ▪ approaching a text	SPEAKING ▪ telling a personal story
2 — REVIEW and PRACTICE		p12				
3 Keep on traveling **3A** p14 **3B** p15 **3C** p16 **3D** p17		▪ comparatives, superlatives, (not) as ... as ▪ past continuous and simple past	▪ sentence stress ▪ was/were	▪ useful adjectives ▪ vacation activities	LISTENING ▪ identifying key points	WRITING ▪ writing a narrative
3 — REVIEW and PRACTICE		p18				
4 The working world **4A** p20 **4B** p21 **4C** p22 **4D** p23		▪ will, may and might for predictions ▪ be going to and present continuous	▪ want/won't ▪ going to and want to	▪ jobs ▪ phrases about work	READING ▪ skimming a text	SPEAKING ▪ telephone language
4 — REVIEW and PRACTICE		p24				
5 Mind and body **5A** p26 **5B** p27 **5C** p28 **5D** p29		▪ should/shouldn't ▪ first conditional	▪ should/shouldn't ▪ 'll contraction	▪ health and medicine ▪ verb collocations (do, make, have and take) ▪ emotions and feelings	LISTENING ▪ listening in detail	WRITING ▪ writing an informal e-mail
5 — REVIEW and PRACTICE		p30				
6 Risks and experiences **6A** p32 **6B** p33 **6C** p34 **6D** p35		▪ present perfect with ever and never ▪ second conditional	▪ irregular past participles ▪ sentence stress	▪ phrasal verbs ▪ the natural world	READING ▪ guessing the meaning of words from context	SPEAKING ▪ agreeing and disagreeing
6 — REVIEW and PRACTICE		p36				

Writing practice p74

3

UNIT 1 All about me

LANGUAGE simple present and adverbs and expressions of frequency ■ personality adjectives

1A The only friends you need

1 Here are some words to describe a good friend. Order the words from 1 (very important) to 6 (less important).

honest   funny   patient   nice   polite   generous

Go to Vocabulary practice: personality adjectives, page 136

2 Read the introduction to the text. Are the sentences true (T) or false (F)?
 1 You need lots of friends to be happy. ____
 2 There are four different types of friends. ____
 3 It is important to have different types of friends in your life. ____

3 A ▶ 1.3   Match the types of friends in the box with descriptions 1–4. Listen and check.

The super planner   The party animal   The good listener   The straight talker

B Do you have any friends like these? What type of friend are you?

THE FOUR FRIENDS YOU NEED

We all know that friends are important … but do we have the "right" friends? Dr. Adam Greenberg, a psychologist, doesn't think we need lots of friends to be happy. Instead, he says it's more important to have different types of friends. He believes that there are four types of friends, and they all help us in different ways. So, what are these four friends like?

1 _____
You share everything with these friends and often tell them all your secrets. They're patient when you call them late at night with a problem and never complain when you tell them the same stories, over and over again!

2 _____
These friends know you very well, and they're honest … really honest. They always tell you the truth, even when you don't want to hear it. But this is because they care about you and don't want you to make a mistake and get hurt.

3 _____
These friends are very sociable, and you usually have a good time when you're with them. They're very funny and make you laugh when you're sad. All your friends and family love them, too. With friends like these, life is never boring!

4 _____
These friends are very organized, but they're sometimes a little serious. They hardly ever forget important dates, like your birthday! They're very busy and have lots of things to do every day, but they always find time to have coffee with you.

4 Choose the correct words to complete the sentences. Check your answers in the text.
 1 *Do / Does* we have the "right" friends?
 2 Dr. Greenberg *don't / doesn't* think we need lots of friends to be happy.
 3 He *say / says* it's more important to have different types of friends.
 4 They *don't / doesn't* want you to make a mistake and get hurt.
 5 You usually have a good time when you *is / are* with them.
 6 They hardly ever *forget / forgets* important dates.

simple present and adverbs and expressions of frequency ■ personality adjectives   LANGUAGE 1A

5 A Complete the diagram with the adverbs of frequency in the box.

hardly ever   never   often   usually

100% ──────────────────────────────────── 0%

always   1 _____   2 _____   sometimes   3 _____   4 _____

B Underline the adverbs of frequency in the text and complete the rule. Then read the Grammar box.

Adverbs of frequency go *before / after* most verbs, but they go *before / after* the verb *be*.

Grammar simple present and adverbs and expressions of frequency

Things that are always true:
Does Ahmet *live* in Ankara? No, he *lives* in Istanbul.
Do you *speak* Spanish? Yes, I *speak* a little.

Routines and habits:
How often do you *see* him? I *usually see* him on the weekends.
How often are you late? I'm *never* late!

Look! We also use expressions of frequency for regular routines e.g., *once a week*, *every month*

Go to **Grammar practice:** simple present with adverbs and expressions of frequency, page 112

6 A ▶ 1.5   **Pronunciation:** final *-s/-es* sound Listen and repeat the sentences. Then match the verb endings in **bold** with the sounds: /s/, /z/, or /əz/.

1 She like**s** Italian food. ____   2 He teach**es** at the university. ____   3 My brother know**s** him. ____

B ▶ 1.6   How do you say the verbs? Listen, check, and repeat.

believe**s**   say**s**   change**s**   think**s**   use**s**   want**s**   goe**s**   watch**es**   hope**s**

7 A Add adverbs and expressions of frequency to make sentences about your partner.

She usually takes the bus to work. He takes the bus to the university every day.

1 He/She takes the bus to work/college.
2 He/She goes to bed at 11:00 p.m.
3 He/She is patient.
4 He/She drinks coffee in the mornings.
5 He/She watches movies in English.
6 He/She is late for class.

B Read your sentences to your partner. He/She will tell you if you are correct.

Go to **Communication practice:** Student A, page 158; Student B, page 166

8 Read the text about two friends. Complete the text with the correct form of the verbs in the box.

get   have   not have   invite   like   think

MY BEST FRIEND IS THE EXACT OPPOSITE OF ME
Lots of people ¹_____ I'm really serious, and that I never go out, but that's not true! I'm very hard-working, and my job at the bank is difficult, so I ²_____ much free time. I play the guitar in a jazz group, and we usually practice two or three times a week.
I ³_____ cooking, so I often ⁴_____ people over to my house for dinner. My best friend is Luca. He's the singer in the group, and he's completely different from me. He's a college student and, to be honest, he's a little lazy and hardly ever ⁵_____ to class on time. But he's funny and generous, and we always ⁶_____ a great time when we go out.

9 A Choose a friend and tell your partner his/her name.

B In pairs, use the prompts to ask and answer questions about your friends.

1 What / be / he/she / like?
2 Where / he/she / live?
3 What / he/she / do?
4 Where / he/she / work/study?
5 How often / you / talk to / him/her?
6 What / you / usually / talk about?
7 How often / you / see / him/her?
8 Where / you / meet / him/her?

Write a description of yourself and of someone you know who is the opposite of you.

5

1 SKILLS LISTENING listening for the main idea ■ contractions ■ hobbies and socializing

1B 21st century hobbies

1 Match the activities in the box with pictures a–h.

> get together with friends   go to concerts   bake cupcakes   play chess
> go on social media   collect records   get (some) exercise   shop online

2 In pairs, ask and answer the questions *Do you …?* and *How often do you …?* for the activities in exercise 1.

- **A** *Do you collect records?* **B** *No, I don't.*
- **A** *How often do you get some exercise?* **B** *I go to the gym once or twice a week.*

Go to Vocabulary practice: hobbies and socializing, page 137

Skill   listening for the main idea

It is important to understand the main idea when someone is speaking.
- Think about who is speaking and what he/she is talking about.
- Don't worry if you don't understand all the words.
- Remember that speakers often talk about the main ideas more than once.

3 ▶ 1.8 Read the Skill box. Watch or listen to the beginning of a webshow called *Learning Curve* and check (✓) the main idea.
1. People have less time for socializing today. ☐
2. Many popular hobbies are now online. ☐
3. Old hobbies are becoming popular again. ☐

4 A ▶ 1.8 Watch or listen again. Complete the chart with the online activities Kate mentions.

Traditional activity	Online activity
play team sports	
take cooking classes	
go to a shopping center	
go out to meet new people	

B In pairs, think of more traditional activities that you can now do online.

listening for the main idea ■ contractions ■ hobbies and socializing   **LISTENING**   **SKILLS**   **1B**

5 ▶ 1.9   Watch or listen to the second part of the show. Choose the correct options to complete the sentences about the main ideas.

1 Viktor …
  a plays chess a lot.   b does lots of activities online.   c meets up with friends every day.
2 David …
  a likes computers.   b exercises at home.   c prefers exercising at the gym.
3 Suzie …
  a downloads lots of music.   b prefers to relax at home.   c does her hobby with other people.
4 Rebecca …
  a does lots of activities online.   b doesn't like meeting new people.   c spends lots of time with her family.

6 ▶ 1.9   Watch or listen again. Are the sentences true (T) or false (F)?
1 Viktor plays chess with friends every day. ____
2 David goes to the gym five times a week or more. ____
3 Suzie loves music from the 1980s. ____
4 Rebecca makes videos of her cat. ____
5 Kate only likes traditional hobbies, like rock climbing. ____

7 **A** Ask your classmates the questions in the boxes and write down their answers.

   What do you do in your free time?   Do you have any online hobbies?

B Do you think online hobbies are more popular than traditional hobbies?

8 ▶ 1.10   In pairs, complete the sentences from the show with the contractions in the box. Listen and check.

   don't   I'm   he's   that's   what's   can't

1 _____ your name?
2 _____ really enjoying the game.
3 Computers _____ interest me.
4 You _____ do that online!
5 I use it when _____ not at the gym.
6 Wow, Suzie, _____ amazing!

Listening builder   contractions

When people speak, they usually make contractions:
We do not get together with friends. → We **don't** get together with friends.
She is not very athletic. → She**'s not** very athletic. / She **isn't** very athletic.
I am ready to go rock climbing. → **I'm** ready to go rock climbing.

9 ▶ 1.11   Read the Listening builder. Listen and circle the contractions you hear.
1 We're / We aren't / We can't
2 He's / He isn't / He doesn't
3 My teacher's / My teacher's not / My teacher isn't
4 It's / It isn't / It doesn't
5 They don't / They can't / They aren't
6 I'm / I'm not / I don't

10 Discuss the questions in pairs.
1 Is it important to have a hobby? Why/Why not?
2 What hobbies are most popular in your country?
3 Do men and women usually like different hobbies?
4 Are your hobbies different now from when you were a child? If so, how?
5 Can you think of any dangerous hobbies? Would you like to try them? Why/Why not?

Personal Best   Write a paragraph about one of your partner's answers in exercise 10.

1 LANGUAGE — present continuous and simple present ■ useful verbs

1C Famous families

1 Who are musicians a–c? In pairs, match them with their relatives: Anaïs, Skip, and Eve. Read the text and check.

THE NEXT GENERATION OF STARS

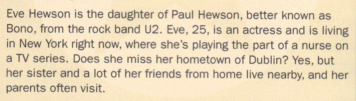

Their faces may look familiar, but if you're wondering who these cool young people are, the clue is in their names. Meet the children—and grandchildren—of some of music's biggest stars.

Anaïs Gallagher is the daughter of Noel Gallagher, former guitarist and songwriter with Oasis. In our photo, she's wearing a gold hat and already looks like a star! Anaïs, 16, goes to school in London and is currently hosting a music and fashion show on children's TV. She lives in London with her mom and, in the future, she wants to be a movie director.

Skip Marley wears his hair in dreadlocks and looks just like his famous grandfather, Bob. He's just 20, but he's also a musician who sings and plays the guitar, the piano, and the drums. He lives in Miami, where he's studying business administration in college. Right now, he's recording some new songs and planning to go on tour.

Eve Hewson is the daughter of Paul Hewson, better known as Bono, from the rock band U2. Eve, 25, is an actress and is living in New York right now, where she's playing the part of a nurse on a TV series. Does she miss her hometown of Dublin? Yes, but her sister and a lot of her friends from home live nearby, and her parents often visit.

With so much talent—never mind those famous connections—we can expect to see a lot more of Anaïs, Skip, and Eve in the future.

Anaïs

Skip

Eve

2 Read the text again. Complete the sentences with the correct name: *Anaïs, Skip,* or *Eve*.

1 _____ lives in Miami.
2 _____ is wearing a white hat in the photo.
3 _____ goes to school in London.
4 _____ is living in New York right now.
5 _____'s parents often visit.
6 _____ is recording some new songs right now.

3 A <u>Underline</u> the verbs in exercise 2. Which verbs are simple present and which are present continuous? What is the difference between them?

B Choose the correct tenses to complete the rules. Then read the Grammar box.

1 We use the *simple present / present continuous* to talk about actions that are happening now or actions that are temporary.
2 We use the *simple present / present continuous* to talk about things that happen regularly or things that are always true.

📖 Grammar — present continuous and simple present

Things that are happening now or are temporary:
She's **living** in Lima right now.
I'**m not wearing** my glasses.
Is she **working** in Paris today?

Things that happen regularly or are always true:
He **lives** in Istanbul.
They **don't wear** coats in the summer.
Do you **work** as a teacher?

Go to Grammar practice: present continuous and simple present, page 113

present continuous and simple present ■ useful verbs   LANGUAGE 1C

4 **A** ▶1.13 **Pronunciation:** *-ng* sound Listen and repeat the words. Pay attention to the /ŋ/ sound.

bri**ng**ing meeti**ng** running si**ng**ing studyi**ng** so**ng** taki**ng** you**ng**

B ▶1.14 Practice saying the sentences. Listen, check, and repeat.
1 She's weari**ng** a lo**ng** coat.
2 She's carryi**ng** a lo**ng** coat.
3 He's bri**ng**ing me a stro**ng** cup of coffee.
4 He's taki**ng** a stro**ng** cup of coffee to the meeti**ng**.

5 Match the sentences in exercise 4B with pictures a–d.

a

b

c

d

Go to Vocabulary practice: useful verbs, page 138

6 **A** Choose the correct form of the verb to complete the questions.
1 What clothes *do you wear / are you wearing* today?
2 *Do you have / Are you having* a dictionary with you?
3 What *do you look forward to / are you looking forward to* this year?
4 *Do you think / Are you thinking* it will rain today?
5 What clothes *do you usually wear / are you usually wearing* if you go to a party?
6 What *do you do / are you doing* right now?

B In pairs, ask and answer the questions.

Go to Communication practice: Student A, page 158; Student B, page 166

7 ▶1.16 Complete the conversation with the simple present or present continuous forms of the verbs in the box. Listen and check.

meet   work (x2)   be   do (x2)   write   not know   not join

Ruben Karen!
Karen Hi, Ruben. How ¹ _____ you?
Ruben I'm fine, thanks. What ² _____ you _____ here?
Karen I ³ _____ my sister for lunch at a café.
Ruben Oh, great. What ⁴ _____ she _____?
Karen She ⁵ _____ at a bank.
Ruben Here downtown?
Karen Not normally, but she ⁶ _____ at the main office this week. Hey, why ⁷ _____ you _____ us for lunch?
Ruben OK, but your sister ⁸ _____ me.
Karen Don't worry. It'll be fine. So, how's college?
Ruben Good, but I'm really busy. I ⁹ _____ my senior project right now, so …

8 Imagine you meet your partner on the street. Ask and answer the questions in pairs.
1 How are you?
2 What are you doing here?
3 Where are you working/living right now?
4 How's it going?
5 How's your …?
6 What does he/she do?
7 What's he/she like?
8 What's he/she doing now?

Personal Best Write about someone in your family with the simple present and present continuous.

9

1 SKILLS WRITING — making notes ■ expressing reasons and results

1D Me in three objects

1 Read the blog and look at the pictures. Discuss the questions in pairs.

1. What can you find out about Sasha, Brady, and Julio?
2. Who do you think is the most interesting?
3. Who do you think is most similar to you?
4. Is it possible to know what someone is like by looking at the things he/she owns?

2 Look at the mind map. Who drew it: Sasha, Brady, or Julio? Complete the diagram with the correct objects. Then read the Skill box.

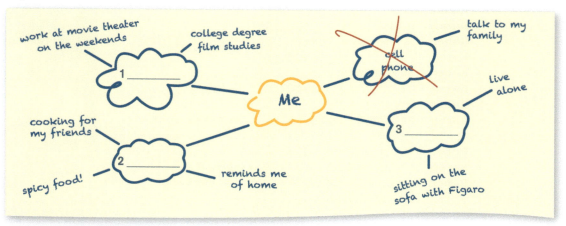

Skill | making notes

Making notes before you write is a good way to plan your work.
- Write as many ideas as you can about the main topics.
- Use diagrams like mind maps to see the ideas more clearly.
- Choose the best ideas and organize them into paragraphs.

making notes ■ expressing reasons and results **WRITING** **SKILLS** **1D**

3 A Look at the mind map again. Which idea doesn't Julio use? How many paragraphs do you think he'll write?

B Read Julio's blog post in exercise 4 and check your answers to the questions above.

4 ▶ 1.17 Complete Julio's blog post with the simple present or present continuous form of the verbs in the box. Listen and check.

> not agree   love   cook   work   live   sit   watch   study

Julio's blog

First, I chose a photo of Figaro, my cat, because he's very important to me. I ¹_____ alone right now, so it is good to see a friendly face when I come home. I ²_____ animals, especially cats. In the photo, he ³_____ on the sofa with me. He often sits with me, and we watch movies together.

I ⁴_____ at a college in the U.S. now, but I'm from Mexico. That's why I also chose Mexican food. I love spicy food, and I often ⁵_____ a big meal and invite all my friends over for dinner. It's great to get together with friends and, when I taste the food, I remember my friends and family back home.

I chose some movie tickets, because I work at a local movie theater on the weekends. I ⁶_____ on a degree in film studies, so movies are a really important part of my life. Some people say I ⁷_____ too many movies, but I ⁸_____ . I want to be a movie director, and I learn something new from every movie I watch.

5 Look at the phrases with the highlighted words in the text. Answer the questions.
1 What type of information comes after *because*? *a reason for something / a result*
2 What type of information comes after *That's why* and *so*? *a reason for something / a result*

Text builder   expressing reasons and results

Reasons: *I chose a photo of my cat **because** he's very important to me.*
Results: *My cat is very important to me, **so** I chose a photo of him.*
              *My cat is very important to me. **That's why** I chose a photo of him.*

---

6 A Read the Text builder. Complete the sentences *with because, so, or That's why!*
1 I think it's really important to stay in shape, _____ I go running every morning.
2 I didn't choose my cell phone _____ everybody has one, and it's not very special.
3 I design websites and I'm always connected to the Internet. _____ I chose my laptop.
4 My backpack is important to me _____ it reminds me of my trips to lots of countries.
5 I love art, but I'm too shy to take a picture of one of my paintings. _____ I chose my paints, instead.

B Who wrote the sentences: Sasha, Brady, or Julio?

7 A Complete the sentences with your own ideas. Write three true sentences and three false sentences.
1 My favorite _____ is _____ because …
2 I think _____ is very _____ , so I …
3 I'm a very _____ person. That's why I never …
4 It's really important to _____ , so I always …
5 I am _____ right now because …
6 I'm terrified of _____ . That's why …

B Listen to your partner's sentences. Which sentences do you think are true?

8 A PREPARE Draw a mind map of some objects that represent you. Then add reasons why the things are special. Look at your diagram and choose three objects you want to include in your blog post.

B PRACTICE Write a blog post with the heading *Me in three objects*. Use your notes from Stage A to help you organize the paragraphs.

C PERSONAL BEST Exchange blog posts with your partner. Read his/her work and correct any mistakes. How could they improve it?

Personal Best   Write six sentences with *because, so,* and *That's why* about your friends, family and hobbies.

11

UNIT 2

Stories and pictures

LANGUAGE simple past and time expressions ■ -ed/-ing adjectives

2A That's me in the photo!

1 A Look at the photos in the text below and say what is happening. What do you call these types of photos?

B Read the text quickly. Match descriptions 1–3 with photos a–c.

the STORY OF selfies

The "age of selfies" began in the early 21st century when people started using smartphones with digital cameras. We now take over a million selfies every day! Here are three interesting selfies with their stories:

1 Robert Cornelius made the world's first "selfie" when he experimented with a camera in 1839. He tried to take a photo of himself, but early cameras worked very slowly, so Robert didn't move for one minute and he couldn't smile. That's why the final photo wasn't very exciting!

2 This terrifying selfie is of Alexander Remnev, from Russia. In May 2014, Alexander traveled to Dubai with a friend. They weren't interested in taking normal photos, so they decided to climb the Princess Tower, which is over 400 m. tall. They opened a door at the top of the building and climbed out … and they didn't use any safety equipment. Why did they do it? They said they were bored!

3 Teenager Jack Surgenor was very excited when he saw Queen Elizabeth II in Northern Ireland on June 24, 2014. He quickly took a selfie and sent it to all his friends. He was very pleased, but how did the Queen feel about being in someone else's photo? We don't know, but she looked a little annoyed!

2 Read the text again. Complete the sentences with the names in the box.

Alexander Remnev   Jack Surgenor   Queen Elizabeth II   Robert Cornelius

1 _____ took a very dangerous photo.
2 _____ wasn't happy to be in a photo.
3 _____ waited a long time to take the photo.
4 _____ took a photo of a famous person.

3 A Write the simple past form of the verbs. Check your answers in the text.

1 begin _____
2 make _____
3 try _____
4 work _____
5 travel _____
6 decide _____
7 be _____ / _____
8 send _____

B Which verbs are regular and which are irregular?

simple past and time expressions ■ -ed/-ing adjectives **LANGUAGE 2A**

4 Underline all the simple past negative sentences and questions in the text. Complete the rules, then read the Grammar box.
1 To form a negative in the simple past, we normally use _____ + the base form .
2 To form a question in the simple past, we normally use _____ + subject + the base form .
3 The negative of was/were is _____ / _____ and the negative of could is _____ .

> **Grammar** simple past and time expressions
>
> | | Regular verbs | Irregular verbs |
> |---|---|---|
> | Positive: | Alexander **traveled** to Dubai. | He **took** a photo. |
> | Negative: | Alexander **didn't travel** to Dubai. | He **didn't take** a photo. |
> | Questions: | Why **did** he **travel** to Dubai? | Why **did** he **take** a photo? |
>
> **Look!** Time expressions go at the end or at the beginning of sentences:
> Alexander traveled to Dubai **in May 2014**. **In May 2014**, Alexander traveled to Dubai.

Go to Grammar practice: simple past and time expressions, page 114

5 A ▶ 2.3 **Pronunciation: -ed endings** Listen to three phrases from the text. Say how the -ed endings are pronounced: /t/, /əd/, or /d/.
1 People start**ed** using smartphones.   2 They open**ed** a door.   3 Early cameras work**ed** very slowly.

B ▶ 2.4 Say how the -ed endings of the verbs are pronounced: /t/, /d/ or /əd/. Listen, check, and repeat.
climb**ed**   decid**ed**   experiment**ed**   look**ed**   travel**ed**   watch**ed**

Go to Communication practice: Student A, page 158; Student B, page 166

6 A Choose the correct adjectives to complete the sentences. Check your answers in the text.
1 That's why the final photo wasn't very *excited / exciting*!
2 This *terrified / terrifying* selfie is of Alexander Remnev, from Russia.
3 They said they were *bored / boring*!
4 Teenager Jack Surgenor was very *excited / exciting* when he saw Queen Elizabeth II.

B Look at sentences 1–4 again and answer the questions.
1 Which adjectives describe people's feelings? _____ , _____
2 Which adjectives describe someone/something that causes a feeling? _____ , _____
3 How many more -ed and -ing adjectives can you find in the text? _____

Go to Vocabulary practice: -ed/-ing adjectives, page 139

7 A Complete the questions with the simple past of the verbs in parentheses.
When was the last time you …
1 _____ embarrassed? (feel)
2 _____ terrified? (be)
3 _____ something tiring? (do)
4 _____ something interesting? (eat)
5 _____ some surprising news? (receive)
6 _____ annoyed with your best friend? (get)

B In pairs, ask and answer the questions and explain what happened.

8 Think about a selfie or photo you took. Ask and answer the questions in pairs.
1 When did you take the photo?
2 Where were you?
3 What did you do?
4 Why did you take the photo?
5 How did you feel?
6 Did you send the photo to anyone?

Personal Best Write down three important dates. Then write sentences explaining what happened and why they are important.

13

2 SKILLS READING approaching a text ■ sequencers

2B Party like it's 1829

1 Describe the picture of a party. Discuss the questions in pairs.
1 Why do people have parties?
2 What do you usually do when you go to a party?
3 Do you prefer to organize parties or to be a guest?
4 What's the worst thing about parties?

> **Skill   approaching a text**
>
> **Before you read a text, predict as much information as you can.**
> • Read the title of the text. Can you guess what it means?
> • Look at the pictures. What people, places, and things do they show?
> • Read the headings of the different sections. What do you think they are about?

2 A Read the Skill box. Try to predict the answers to the questions about the text on page 15.
1 Who was Andrew Jackson?
2 Where did he live?
3 What did the guests do at the 1829 party?
4 What did the guests do at the 1837 party?

B Read the whole text quickly and check your answers to the questions.

3 Read the text in more detail. Look at the sentences and write: *1829 party*, *1837 party*, or *both*.
1 There was food at the party. _____
2 Some guests caused damage. _____
3 All the guests had a good time. _____
4 Jackson didn't stay until the end. _____
5 Jackson received a strange present. _____
6 The guests ate in the gardens. _____

4 Discuss the questions in pairs.
1 Were you surprised by the text? Why/Why not?
2 How would a party at the White House be different today?
3 What kind of person was Andrew Jackson?
4 Would you like to go to a party like one of Andrew Jackson's? Why/Why not?

5 Complete the sentences with the words in the box. Check your answers in the text.

> after   after that   later   then

1 ... they soon pushed their way inside. _____ , the party got out of control.
2 Eight years _____ , a farmer gave the president an enormous cheese.
3 Jackson didn't know what to do with it; he couldn't eat it himself, but _____ he had an idea.
4 _____ just two hours, he checked and it was gone.

> **Text builder   sequencers**
>
> **To say one action happened after another:**
> *I went to the gym and **then** I went home.*   *I went to the gym. **After that**, I went home.*
> **To say one action happened after a period of time:**
> *Two hours **later**, I cooked dinner.*   ***After** two hours, I cooked dinner.*

6 Read the Text builder. In pairs, talk about an important party or celebration you went to. Use sequencers to explain what happened.
• What was the party or celebration?
• How many guests were there?
• What did you eat and drink?
• What did you do?
• Did you have a good time?
• Were there any problems?

approaching a text ■ sequencers   READING   SKILLS 2B

PARTY LIKE A PRESIDENT

Andrew Jackson was president of the United States from 1829 to 1837. He was the first president from the Democratic party and a very popular politician, but he's also famous for some surprising events that took place at the White House. The pictures below show two memorable parties held there when Jackson was president.

ANDREW JACKSON

THE 1829 CELEBRATIONS

THE LAST PARTY, 1837

On March 4, 1829, when Jackson became president, he invited his supporters to visit the White House, and thousands of people followed him to his new home. At first, the crowd waited in the gardens, but they were very excited and soon pushed their way inside. After that, the party got out of control. People stood on tables and chairs, broke glasses, and some even fell down and hurt themselves. Jackson escaped through a window and went to a nearby hotel, but his staff stayed because they were worried about the building. In the end, they put lots of food on tables in the gardens and the hungry guests followed them outside to eat the food. The White House was safe ... for the moment!

Eight years later, a farmer gave the president an enormous cheese, which weighed over 600 kg. Jackson didn't know what to do with it; he couldn't eat it himself, but then he had an idea. He decided to have another party to celebrate the end of his presidency. In February 1837, thousands of guests arrived and started to eat the only thing on the menu—the cheese. After just two hours, he checked and it was gone. Everyone was very happy, but the expensive carpets in the White House were covered with smelly cheese. This time, Jackson wasn't worried about the mess. He left the White House two weeks later, and the next president, Martin van Buren, was very annoyed because the building still smelled of cheese!

Personal Best Choose one of the parties from the text. Write a summary of what happened.

2 LANGUAGE question forms ■ life stages

2C Behind the camera

1 In pairs, order the stages from 1 (birth) to 8 (death).

> start a career   get engaged   die   go to college
> be born   have children   finish school   get married

Go to Vocabulary practice: life stages, page 140

2 Read the radio guide about Mario Testino. What is his job? Why is he famous?

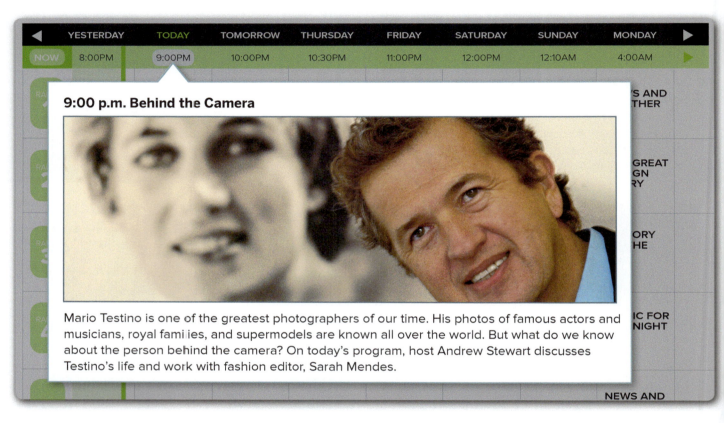

9:00 p.m. Behind the Camera

Mario Testino is one of the greatest photographers of our time. His photos of famous actors and musicians, royal families, and supermodels are known all over the world. But what do we know about the person behind the camera? On today's program, host Andrew Stewart discusses Testino's life and work with fashion editor, Sarah Mendes.

3 ▶ 2.7 Listen to the radio program. Choose the correct options to complete the sentences.
1 Mario was born in *Italy / Peru*.
2 He grew up in *Lima / New York*.
3 After high school, he *went to college / traveled around the world*.
4 In London, he got a job in a *restaurant / hospital*.
5 He started his career by photographing *models and actors / people he worked with*.
6 He became famous when he photographed *Madonna / Gianni Versace*.
7 He photographed Princess Diana in *1995 / 1997*.
8 In 2012, he opened a gallery in *London / Lima*.

4 ▶ 2.8 Complete the host's questions with the words in the box. Listen again and check.

> does   did   from   is   what   who

1 Where is he _____ ?
2 _____ did he do after he finished high school?
3 How _____ his career start?
4 _____ did he work with?
5 What _____ he doing today?
6 _____ he still live in London?

question forms ■ life stages   LANGUAGE 2C

5 Look at exercise 4 again and answer the questions. Then read the Grammar box.
1 Which question doesn't have a question word? _____
2 In questions 1–6, which auxiliary verbs are used for:
   a the simple present?   _____
   b the simple past?   _____
   c the present continuous?   _____
3 Which question doesn't have an auxiliary verb? _____

> **Grammar** question forms
>
> Most verbs: (question word) + auxiliary verb + subject + main verb
>   *Where do you live?*   *Does your brother live near here?*   *What do we know about Mario Testino?*
>   *When did you arrive?*   *Did you see him?*   *How did his career start?*
>   *What are you doing?*   *Is Mario working today?*   *What am I doing?*
>
> The verb *be*:   (question word) + *be* + subject
>   *Where is he from?*   *Was he late for work?*
>
> **Look!** Prepositions don't usually come before the question word: *Who did he work with?* NOT ~~*With who did he work?*~~

Go to Grammar practice: question forms, page 115

6 ▶ 2.11 **Pronunciation:** question intonation Listen to two of the questions from the radio program. Does the intonation go up ↗ or down ↘ at the end of the questions?
1 How did his career start?   up ↗ / down ↘
2 Does he still live in London?   up ↗ / down ↘

7 **A** Put the words in parentheses in the correct place in the questions.
1 Was Mario's father Peru? (from)
2 Why he take Mario to New York? (did)
3 When did move to London? (Mario)
4 Did Princess Diana in 1997? (die)
5 Does live in New York now? (he)
6 What does the radio host play? (song)

B ▶ 2.12 Say the questions with the correct intonation. Listen, check, and repeat. Then ask and answer the questions in pairs.

Go to Communication practice: Student A, page 159; Student B, page 167

8 In pairs, ask and answer questions with the words.

1 you / busy / right now?
2 what time / you / wake up / this morning?
3 you / have / a driver's license?
4 where / you / go on vacation / last year?
5 how often / you / take / photographs?
6 which TV series / you / watch / these days?

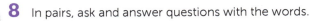

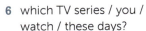

9 Write four sentences about you and your family. Read the sentences to your partner. He/She should ask questions to find out more information.
A *I went to college in São Paulo.*   B *What did you study there?*
A *My father retired last year.*   B *What was his job?*

Personal Best Write five quiz questions about a famous person.

17

2 SKILLS SPEAKING telling a personal story ■ showing interest

2D That reminds me of …

1 ▶ 2.13 Look at the pictures. In pairs, predict what happened on Taylor's first day of work. Watch or listen to the first part of *Learning Curve* and check.

2 ▶ 2.13 Are the sentences true (T) or false (F)? Watch or listen again and check.
1 Taylor's new job is in a fitness center. ____
2 She was worried about being late. ____
3 She arrived at work fifteen minutes early. ____
4 A big car hit her car. ____
5 The man in the car shouted at her. ____
6 She was embarrassed. ____

Conversation builder | **telling a personal story**

Starting the story:
Something similar happened to me.
That reminds me of …
Let me tell you about …

Involving the listener:
You'll never guess … (who it was / what happened next / what she said)
Can you imagine?
But that's not all.

Saying how you felt:
It was so …
I felt really …
At first, I felt …

---

3 ▶ 2.14 Read the Conversation builder. Match the two parts to make sentences that Taylor used in her story. Listen, check, and repeat.
1 Let me tell you about
2 At first, I felt
3 I felt
4 But that's
5 You'll never guess
6 It was so

a embarrassing.
b not all.
c my first day.
d great.
e really angry.
f who took my parking spot.

4 In pairs, write three phrases that Taylor's new boss could use to tell the story of what happened.

18

telling a personal story ■ showing interest **SPEAKING**   SKILLS   **2D**

5 A ▶ 2.15   In pairs, order phrases a–h from Penny's story. Watch or listen to the second part of the show, and check.

- **a** ☐ I sent the message to him by mistake!
- **b** ☐ My boss had the same name as my friend—Steve Jones.
- **c** ☐ He thought it was funny, but can you imagine how I felt?
- **d** ☐ Everyone in the office could hear him! It was quite embarrassing.
- **e** ☐ Something similar happened to me at my last job.
- **f** ☐ You'll never guess what he said. "I'm glad you think I'm handsome and amazing, but it isn't my birthday!"
- **g** ☐ I worked at a radio station in London before I moved to New York.
- **h** ☐ I sent my good friend Steve an e-mail message for his birthday. It said, "Happy birthday to my handsome, amazing friend!"

B ▶ 2.15   Watch or listen again. How are Taylor and Penny's stories similar?

6 ▶ 2.16   Listen and repeat the phrases when you hear the beeps. How do Taylor and Penny show they are interested in each other's stories?

> **Skill   showing interest**
>
> Good listeners show that they are interested in what someone else is saying.
> - Use short response expressions, such as *Oh, no! Really?* etc.
> - Ask questions about what happened.
> - Use the correct intonation to show you are interested.

7 Read the Skill box. Put the phrases in the correct columns.

What happened?   That's amazing!   Really?   What did he do then?
Oh no!   You're kidding!   That's awful!   Lucky you!   You poor thing!   Great!

Responding to something positive	Responding to something negative	Showing interest or asking for more information

8 A ▶ 2.17   Listen to phrases 1–6. Which speaker sounds more interested: A or B?

1 What happened? _____
2 That's amazing! _____
3 Really? _____
4 Oh no, that's awful! _____
5 You're joking! _____
6 Lucky you! _____

B ▶ 2.18   In pairs, say phrases 1–6 to show you are interested. Listen, check, and repeat.

Go to Communication practice: Student A, page 158; Student B, page 166

9 A PREPARE   Choose one of the ideas. Make notes on what happened and how you felt.

your first day at work/school/college

a birthday or celebration

a time when you lost something important

a difficult day

B PRACTICE   In pairs, take turns telling your stories. Listen to your partner and show you are interested by responding to what he/she says or by asking questions.

C PERSONAL BEST   Find another partner and tell your story again. How is your storytelling better this time?

Personal Best   How well did you listen to your partner's story? Write about what happened and how he/she felt.

19

1 and 2 REVIEW and PRACTICE

Grammar

1 Choose the correct options to complete the sentences.

1 _____ married?
 a You are
 b Are you
 c Is you

2 She _____ Japanese food.
 a 's liking
 b like
 c likes

3 _____ take a message?
 a I can
 b Can I
 c Do I can

4 In the summer I _____ .
 a every day go swimming
 b go swimming every day
 c go every day swimming

5 When _____ here?
 a do you got
 b did you get
 c are you get

6 We went to Brazil _____ year.
 a last
 b past
 c ago

7 The train _____ in the morning.
 a late is always
 b always is late
 c is always late

8 _____ time did you wake up yesterday?
 a Which
 b When
 c What

2 Rewrite the sentences using the tenses in parentheses.

1 I work in a restaurant.
 I *worked* in a *restaurant*. (simple past)

2 I don't wear dark clothes.
 I _____ dark clothes. (present continuous)

3 Where do you go to school?
 Where _____ to school? (simple past)

4 What do you do?
 What _____? (present continuous)

5 Did you take a lot of photos on your trip?
 _____ a lot of photos on your trip? (simple present)

6 I buy bread in the supermarket.
 I _____ bread in the supermarket. (simple past)

3 Complete the text with the correct forms of the verbs in parentheses.

Ishita Malaviya

Where [1]_____ (be) Ishita from?

She [2]_____ (grow up) in Mumbai, India and now she [3]_____ (live) in Manipal, in the state of Karnataka, 875 km. away.

What [4]_____ she _____ (do)?

A few years ago, she [5]_____ (become) India's first professional female surfer and now she [6]_____ (have) a sufing school, where she [7]_____ (teach) tourists and local people how to surf.

How [8]_____ she _____ (start) surfing?

When she [9]_____ (go) to college in 2007, she met a German student with a surfboard. At first, she [10]_____ (not can) believe that people surfed in India, so she asked him about it and started to learn.

What [11]_____ she _____ (do) today?

She [12]_____ (make) a movie about her story. She hopes it makes more people want to learn how to surf in India.

Vocabulary

1 Match the adjectives with the definitions.

> shy embarrassed patient annoying confused disappointed lazy generous

Someone who ...

1 feels bad because he/she made a mistake. _____
2 doesn't want to work or try hard. _____
3 is happy to give money, help, or his/her time. _____
4 doesn't mind waiting a long time for something. _____
5 doesn't understand something. _____
6 feels sad because something bad happened. _____
7 doesn't like meeting lots of new people. _____
8 makes other people feel a little angry. _____

REVIEW and PRACTICE 1 and 2

2 Circle the word that is different. Explain your answer.

1	wear	carry	bring	funny
2	rude	tired	honest	sociable
3	boring	excited	interesting	disappointing
4	retire	stay in shape	grow up	finish school
5	tell	expect	remind	nice
6	yoga	Pilates	swimming	exercise
7	get up	get married	get engaged	get a divorce
8	hope	relax	expect	look forward to

3 Choose the correct options to complete the sentences.

1 Thank you for eating at our restaurant. Please _____ soon!
   a go back   b grow up   c come back
2 She really _____ her mother. They have the same eyes.
   a looks   b looks like   c reminds
3 Hayley is really _____. She spends ten hours a day in the office.
   a hard-working   b serious   c patient
4 I _____ the meeting to finish at about 3:00.
   a wait   b expect   c look forward to
5 Can you _____ me your name please?
   a tell   b say   c remember
6 Raul _____ most weekends with his family.
   a joins   b spends   c keeps
7 When I was a child, I _____ swimming every Sunday.
   a went   b did   c played
8 My soccer team lost the game. I feel so _____!
   a excited   b relaxed   c disappointed

4 Complete the sentences with the verbs in the box.

> go on   lose   retire   wait   remember
> learn   have   finish   miss   meet

1 Most students _____ high school at the age of eighteen.
2 Sonia didn't _____ the train, but she arrived late.
3 All my friends _____ social media every day.
4 Did Alex _____ to buy some eggs?
5 My father is 62, and he wants to _____ next year.
6 When you are in college, you _____ lots of interesting people.
7 How often do you _____ your sunglasses?
8 I'm married, but I don't want to _____ any children.
9 This year, I want to _____ to play a musical instrument.
10 Can you _____ for me after class?

Personal Best

Lesson 1A
Describe two friends using personality adjectives.

Lesson 2A
Write two things you did last weekend.

Lesson 1A
Describe one thing you do every month and one thing you do every year.

Lesson 2B
Write a sentence about what you did yesterday using *after*.

Lesson 1B
Name five hobbies or activities you like doing.

Lesson 2C
Write two questions for an interview with a musician you like.

Lesson 1C
Write a sentence using the simple present and present continuous.

Lesson 2C
Think of a relative and describe two of his/her life stages.

Lesson 1D
Write a sentence about yourself using *because*.

Lesson 2D
Give an expression to start telling a story.

Lesson 1D
Write a sentence about someone you know using *so*.

Lesson 2D
Give an expression to show you are interested in a story.

21

UNIT 3
Keep on traveling

LANGUAGE comparatives, superlatives, *(not) as … as* ■ useful adjectives

3A Tourist or traveler?

1 **A** Look at the title of the quiz. What is the difference between a "tourist" and a "traveler"?

B Match the speech bubbles with the people in the pictures.

2 <u>Underline</u> all the adjectives in the speech bubbles.

Go to Vocabulary practice: useful adjectives, page 141

3 **A** Take the quiz in pairs. Write down your partner's answers.

B Look at the results on page 174. Are you and your partner similar?

1 *I want to go to different countries, try unusual food, and have an adventure.*

2 *I prefer to stay at nice hotels, visit famous sights, and have a good time.*

Personal Best

ARE YOU A TOURIST OR A TRAVELER?

1 What do you usually do on vacation?
a I try to see the most famous sights in a city or visit the big museums.
b I like to go somewhere unusual and discover new things.

2 Do you prefer to stay downtown or away from the center of town?
a Downtown can be more expensive, but it's the best place to be.
b I prefer to be farther away from the downtown area. It's cheaper and quieter.

3 Do you use a guidebook?
a Yes, I do. I like to plan my trip carefully before I go.
b Never! Reading guidebooks isn't as good as talking with local people.

4 Do you ever explore new places alone?
a No, I don't. Vacations are about spending time with friends and family.
b Yes, I do. You discover more about yourself when you're by yourself.

5 What time of year do you prefer to travel?
a In the summer, when the weather is hot and everyone is happier.
b The summer is the worst time! Places aren't as crowded at other times of the year.

a

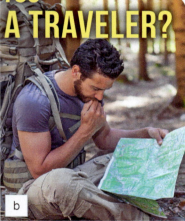
b

4 Complete the chart with comparative and superlative adjectives from the quiz. Can you complete the other forms?

	famous	cheap	happy	far	good	bad
comparative						
superlative	*the most famous*					

5 Match sentences 1–2 with the correct meanings a–b. Then read the Grammar box.

1 Reading guidebooks isn't as good as talking with local people. ____
2 Reading guidebooks is as good as talking with local people. ____

a Reading guidebooks and talking with to local people are equally good.
b Reading guidebooks is worse than talking with local people.

22

comparatives, superlatives, (not) as … as ■ useful adjectives   **LANGUAGE 3A**

Grammar comparatives, superlatives, (not) as … as

Comparatives:
Your hotel is **cheaper** than my hotel.
The festival is **more exciting** than the castle.

Superlatives:
This is **the biggest** museum in the country.
The castle is **the most famous** building in the city.

(not) as … as:
The beaches are**n't as crowded as** they are in the summer.

Go to Grammar practice: comparatives, superlatives, (not) as … as, page 116

6 ▶ 3.3 Listen to Michelle ask three friends for advice. Check (✓) the advice they recommend.

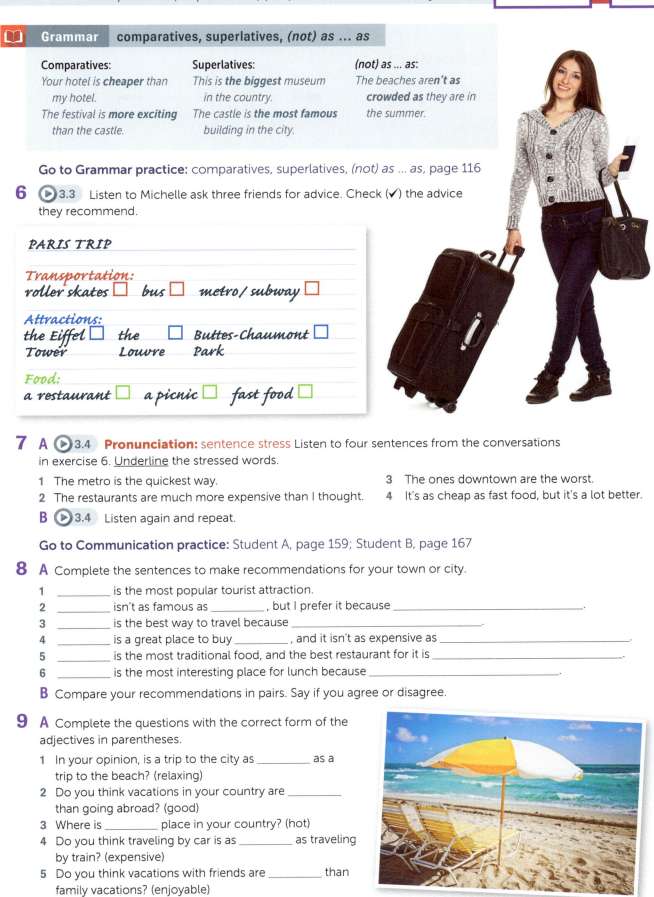

PARIS TRIP

Transportation:
roller skates ☐   bus ☐   metro/subway ☐

Attractions:
the Eiffel ☐   the ☐   Buttes-Chaumont ☐
Tower   Louvre   Park

Food:
a restaurant ☐   a picnic ☐   fast food ☐

7 A ▶ 3.4 **Pronunciation: sentence stress** Listen to four sentences from the conversations in exercise 6. Underline the stressed words.

1 The metro is the quickest way.
2 The restaurants are much more expensive than I thought.
3 The ones downtown are the worst.
4 It's as cheap as fast food, but it's a lot better.

B ▶ 3.4 Listen again and repeat.

Go to Communication practice: Student A, page 159; Student B, page 167

8 A Complete the sentences to make recommendations for your town or city.
1 _____ is the most popular tourist attraction.
2 _____ isn't as famous as _____ , but I prefer it because _____.
3 _____ is the best way to travel because _____.
4 _____ is a great place to buy _____ , and it isn't as expensive as _____.
5 _____ is the most traditional food, and the best restaurant for it is _____.
6 _____ is the most interesting place for lunch because _____.

B Compare your recommendations in pairs. Say if you agree or disagree.

9 A Complete the questions with the correct form of the adjectives in parentheses.
1 In your opinion, is a trip to the city as _____ as a trip to the beach? (relaxing)
2 Do you think vacations in your country are _____ than going abroad? (good)
3 Where is _____ place in your country? (hot)
4 Do you think traveling by car is as _____ as traveling by train? (expensive)
5 Do you think vacations with friends are _____ than family vacations? (enjoyable)
6 In your opinion, what is _____ thing about a vacation? (bad)

B Ask and answer the questions in pairs. Try to give more information.

Personal Best Choose three places and make sentences about them with comparatives, superlatives, and (not) as … as.

23

3 SKILLS LISTENING identifying key points ■ sentence stress ■ vacation activities

3B Staycation or vacation?

1 Match the activities in the box with the pictures. Which activities do you usually do on vacation?

> sunbathe   visit a museum   go sightseeing   buy souvenirs
> rent a car   eat out   go abroad   stay at a hotel

Go to Vocabulary practice: vacation activities, page 138

2 Discuss the questions in pairs.
1 How often do you take a vacation?
2 Do you ever go abroad? Why/Why not?
3 Where do you usually stay?
4 Who do you usually go with?
5 What do you enjoy doing most on vacation?
6 What is the worst thing about a vacation?

3 3.8 Guess the correct definition of a "staycation". Watch or listen to the first part of *Learning Curve* and check.

A "staycation" is a vacation where you stay …
a in your country.   b at your own home.   c at a friend's house.

🔧 Skill   Identifying key points

When people speak, listen for the important things they say.
- They usually emphasize the most important ideas.
- After an important idea, they sometimes give an example or more information.
- Find the key words in the questions and listen very carefully when the speaker talks about them.

4 ▶ 3.7 Read the Skill box. Watch or listen again and check (✓) the key points Penny mentions.
1 Vacations need a lot of planning. ☐
2 They can be expensive. ☐
3 Hotels are great for relaxing. ☐
4 Travel can be tiring. ☐
5 You don't have to travel on a staycation. ☐
6 You can go to your favorite places. ☐
7 You can relax at home. ☐
8 You can continue your daily routine. ☐

5 ▶ 3.8 Watch or listen to the second part of the show. Check (✓) the type of vacation the people are having.
1 Terry and Carol   staycation ☐ vacation ☐
2 Ayoku   staycation ☐ vacation ☐
3 Lisa   staycation ☐ vacation ☐

24

identifying key points ■ sentence stress ■ vacation activities **LISTENING** **SKILLS** **3B**

6 ▶ 3.8 Watch or listen again. Are the sentences true (T) or false (F)?
1 Terry and Carol are having a bad time on holiday. ____
2 They're in Ireland. ____
3 They think staycations can be boring. ____
4 Ayoku has two weeks off work. ____
5 He wants to spend the time relaxing in his apartment. ____
6 Last year he went on vacation, but didn't relax much. ____
7 Lisa's cousins have come to visit her in New York. ____
8 She prefers to show them popular tourist attractions. ____

Terry and Carol

Ayoku

Lisa

7 Discuss the questions about your last vacation in pairs.

Where did you go? Where did you stay? What did you eat? What did you do? What was the weather like? Did you have a good time? Who did you go with?

Listening builder sentence stress

English speakers usually stress the most important words in a sentence. You can usually understand the general idea if you only hear these words.
A **staycation** is a **vacation** where you **stay** at your **own home**.
You can **make time** to **eat out** at your **favorite restaurant** or **drive** to the **beach**.

8 A Read the Listening builder. Look at the words in the sentences 1–5 from the show. Can you understand the general ideas?
1 _____ hired _____ car _____ came _____ _____ lovely national park!
2 _____ usually stay _____ home _____ _____ often boring.
3 _____ doing all _____ things _____ don't usually _____ time _____ do.
4 _____ _____ actually _____ stressful _____ everything _____ planned.
5 _____ _____ family visits, _____ take _____ _____ places _____ many tourists never see.

B ▶ 3.9 In pairs, try to complete the sentences with the unstressed words. Listen and check.

9 Discuss the questions in pairs. Give reasons for your answers.
Which is better...

1 sunbathing or going sightseeing?

3 flying or traveling by train?

2 staying at a hotel or going camping?

4 packing a big suitcase or taking a small backpack?

Personal Best Write a paragraph explaining to tourists what there is to do in your town or city.

3 LANGUAGE past continuous and simple past

3C A traveler's tale

1 A Read the introduction to the text and look at the pictures. Answer the questions in pairs.

1. How long do you think Alastair's trip took?
2. How many countries do you think he visited?
3. What type of problems do you think he had on the trip?
4. What kind of person do you think Alastair is?
5. Would you like to go on an adventure like this? Why/Why not?

B Read the rest of the text and check your answers.

Around the world by bike

In 2001, Alastair Humphreys was studying to become a teacher, but he really wanted to do something different. A few months later, he surprised his friends and family by beginning an amazing trip that took him around the world … on his bike!

In all, Alastair visited 60 countries and, throughout the trip, he kept a blog to record all of his experiences. Although there were some special moments on the road, there was also disappointment and disaster. One disappointment came early. Alastair's dream was to ride his bike all the way, except for taking ships to cross the oceans. Unfortunately, this was impossible. The police stopped him while he was traveling through Egypt, and he had to ride in the back of a truck. He was angry, but there was no other way to continue.

The rest of the time, he rode, rode, rode. On one occasion, his bike broke down while he was crossing the Arizona desert. Help came from a surprising place. To his amazement, complete strangers bought him a new bike so that he could continue his incredible journey.

The trip was tough, and Alastair didn't have enough money to stay at nice hotels. While he was riding through Patagonia, he didn't take a shower for 24 days!
However, one of the hardest parts of his trip came when he traveled through Russia in the winter. Luckily, a friend joined him, so he wasn't traveling alone. But it was so cold that Alistair's beard froze while they were traveling through Siberia.
But none of these problems could stop him from completing the trip. Four years and 75,000 km. later, Alastair finally arrived back home in the U.K. with lots of stories to tell.

2 In pairs, answer the questions. Read the text again and check your answers.

1. Why didn't he ride his bike the whole time?
2. How did he get a new bike?
3. What were his accommodations like?
4. Where did he experience the worst weather?

3 A Complete the sentences with the correct verbs. Check your answers in the text.

1. He _____ the Arizona desert when his bike _____ down.
2. While they _____ their bikes through Siberia, Alastair's beard _____ .

B Look at the sentences again and answer the questions. Then read the Grammar box.

1. Which verbs describe completed actions in the past? _____ , _____
2. Which verbs describe actions happening at the time of the completed action? _____ , _____

past continuous and simple past   LANGUAGE 3C

Grammar past continuous and simple past

Actions in progress at a time in the past:
In 2001, Alastair Humphreys **was studying** to become a teacher.

Actions in progress when a completed action happened:
The police **stopped** him while he **was traveling** through Egypt.
He **was traveling** through Egypt when the police **stopped** him.

Go to Grammar practice: past continuous and simple past, page 117

4 A ▶ 3.11 **Pronunciation:** *was/were* Listen to the sentences and underline the stressed words. How do you pronounce *was* and *were*?

1 I was driving home at 6:00 yesterday evening.
2 They were working hard when I got to the office.
3 It didn't rain while Anita was staying in Seattle.
4 What were you doing at 8:00 this morning?

B Practice saying the sentences in pairs.

5 In pairs, ask and answer the question *What were you doing …?* using the time in each of the boxes. Pay attention to how you say *was* and *were*.

| in 2014 | at 7:30 this morning | this time last week |
| one hour ago | yesterday evening at 6:00 | last year |

6 A Look at the pictures. Complete the sentences with your own ideas.

1 I was sleeping in bed when …

3 While Barbara was cooking dinner, …

2 They were running in the park when …

4 My boss called me while …

B Compare your answers in pairs.

Go to Communication practice: Student A, page 160; Student B, page 168

7 ▶ 3.12 Choose the correct form of the verbs to complete the conversation. Listen and check.

David Did I ever tell you about how I [1]*met / was meeting* a museum guide in Boston?
Emma No, I don't think so.
David It was in 2012. While I [2]*traveled / was traveling* around the U.S., I [3]*waited / was waiting* for a train to New York City, but I was hungry, so I [4]*went / was going* to a café to buy a sandwich. While I [5]*sat / was sitting* there, a man at another table [6]*got up / was getting up* and [7]*left / was leaving* his wallet.
Emma Oh no! What did you do?
David I [8]*ran / was running* after him and [9]*gave / was giving* him the wallet back. But the funny thing is, when I [10]*got / was getting* to the platform later, the same man [11]*waited / was waiting* for the train.
Emma Really?
David Yes, and he [12]*was / was being* a museum guide at the Museum of Natural History in New York City. He [13]*offered / was offering* to show me around to thank me for returning his wallet. The museum was amazing!

8 Think about a vacation or travel experience you had. Discuss the questions in pairs.

1 Where and when did you go?
2 What were the best/worst moments?
3 What were you doing when the best/worst moments happened?

Personal Best Describe an important event in your life. Use the simple past and past continuous to explain what happened.

3 SKILLS WRITING writing a narrative ■ adverbs of manner

3D Travel problems

1 Discuss the questions in pairs.
1 When was the last time you were at an airport?
2 Why were you there?
3 How do you usually feel when you are at an airport?
4 What problems can happen at an airport?

2 ▶ 3.13 Look at pictures a–f and order them from 1–6. Listen and check.

3 ▶ 3.13 Complete the text with the correct form of the verbs in the box. Listen again and check.

arrive   book   buy   have   open   carry   receive   run   see   wait

In 2013, Martin Hendon was living in London. One morning, he ¹_____ a quick breakfast, when he ²_____ a letter from his best friend, Tony. It was an invitation to Tony's wedding … in Naples, Italy, in two weeks! So Martin quickly ³_____ a flight and ⁴_____ a new suit.

The day before the wedding didn't start well. Martin ⁵_____ patiently at the airport when he ⁶_____ that his flight was canceled. He caught a later flight that night and arrived in Naples early the next morning, but he was very tired and accidentally took the wrong suitcase. When he ⁷_____ it up in his hotel room, he found someone else's clothes!

He ⁸_____ down the street desperately looking for a new suit, but it was Sunday and the stores were still closed. Just then, he recognized a passenger from his plane walking slowly down the street. She ⁹_____ a suitcase the same color as Martin's. He asked her politely to open it, and there was Martin's new suit inside!

He changed his clothes and took a taxi to the wedding. When Martin ¹⁰_____ , he opened the door nervously. Inside, everyone was waiting for the wedding to begin. Tony looked at him and smiled. He was only a few minutes late.

4 Match the paragraphs from exercise 3 with descriptions a–d. Then read the Skill box.

Paragraph 1   a the problem (what happened)
Paragraph 2   b the resolution (how he solved the problem)
Paragraph 3   c the background (who, when, where)
Paragraph 4   d the ending (what happened in the end, how he felt)

🔧 Skill   writing a narrative

When you write a story, make it easy to follow and interesting.
- Tell the story in chronological order.
- Organize your ideas into four paragraphs (the background, the problem, the resolution, the ending).
- Use adjectives and adverbs to make the text more interesting.

writing a narrative ■ adverbs of manner **WRITING** **SKILLS** **3D**

5 **A** Complete the sentences from Martin's story. Check your answers in the text.
   1 One morning, he was having a _____ breakfast.   2 Martin _____ booked a flight.
   B Answer the questions about sentences 1 and 2.
   1 Which word is an adjective and describes a noun? _____
   2 Which word is an adverb and describes a verb? _____
   3 What letters do we add to most adjectives to make an adverb? _____

6 Underline seven more adverbs that describe verbs in Martin's story.

> **Text builder**   adverbs of manner
>
> We use adverbs of manner to say how someone does an action:
> Martin was waiting **patiently** at the airport.
> Most adjectives: quiet → quietly, slow → slowly
> Adjectives ending in -y: happy → happily, angry → angrily
> Irregular adverbs: good → well, fast → fast, hard → hard
>
> **Look!** Adverbs of manner come at the end of the phrase:
> He speaks Spanish **well**. NOT ~~He speaks well Spanish~~.

7 Read the Text builder. Choose the correct words to complete the first paragraph of another story.

> Ana Carvalho is from Goiânia, Brazil, but in 2015, she was living in São Paulo where she was studying ¹hard / hardly in college. After her exams, she was waiting ²nervous / nervously for the results, but she was also very ³happy / happily because it was her birthday in two days.
>
> She planned to go home to celebrate with her friends and family in Goiânia. Ana was very ⁴practical / practically, and the night before the flight she packed her suitcase ⁵careful / carefully, checked to make sure she had her passport and tickets, and slept ⁶good / well.

8 **A** **PREPARE** Match phrases 1–6 with pictures a–f. In pairs, discuss what happened to Ana Carvalho. Put your ideas into three groups for the next three paragraphs of the narrative.
   1 apologize and give her a ticket to Goiânia ____   4 receive the exam results at her party ____
   2 begin to worry on the plane ____   5 not hear her correctly ____
   3 realize that the plane is flying to Guyana ____   6 ask which gate is for Goiânia ____

B **PRACTICE** Use your notes to help you write the rest of Ana's story. Remember to use adverbs.

C **PERSONAL BEST** Exchange stories with another pair. Check (✓) three sentences that are well-written.

Personal Best   Write five sentences about a vacation experience you had. Use a different adverb in each sentence.

29

UNIT 4 The working world

LANGUAGE *will*, *may*, and *might* for predictions ■ jobs

4A The future of work

1 A Look at the title of the text and the picture. What do you think it is about?

B In pairs, decide which jobs machines will do in the future and which jobs will always need people.

> accountant   fashion designer   farmer   journalist   model   police officer
> receptionist   salesperson   surgeon   tour guide   waiter/waitress

Go to Vocabulary practice: jobs, page 142

2 Read the text. Which jobs do experts think that machines will do?

WILL A ROBOT TAKE MY JOB?

I'm at the Henn-na Hotel in Japan. A well-dressed Japanese woman welcomes me and asks if I have a reservation. But this is no ordinary receptionist. She is, in fact, a robot—one of several at the hotel that can carry your bags to your room, and even give you travel tips.

Robots and computers are taking our jobs. According to experts, ninety years from now, machines will replace 70% of today's occupations. Accountants and telephone salespeople may be the first to lose their jobs. In restaurants, robots might replace waiters and waitresses. Models might also disappear; fashion designer, Ralph Lauren, is already experimenting with holographic models for his clothes. And in the future, when you go to the hospital for an operation, even the surgeon probably won't be real.

So, should we be worried? The answer is no. History shows us that as old jobs die, new jobs replace them. So, what jobs will exist for us in the future? Here are our top three predictions:

1 Drone controller
Drones will deliver our groceries, remove our trash, and may even act as police officers. But people will still need to control these flying devices from the ground.

2 Vertical farmer
Transporting food will probably become more expensive, and with crowded cities, there will only be one way to grow food and vegetables—upward! Supermarkets will grow all their food above them in special glass buildings.

3 Space tour guide
In the future, people won't want to travel around the world on vacation. Space tourism will create thousands of jobs for space pilots and tour guides to take tourists out of this world!

3 Match the two columns to make complete sentences. Check your answers in the text.

1 Ninety years from now, machines will
2 Accountants and telephone salespeople may
3 Models might
4 The surgeon probably won't
5 Transporting food will probably
6 People won't

a become more expensive.
b also disappear.
c want to travel around the world on vacation.
d replace 70% of today's occupations.
e be the first to lose their jobs.
f be real.

4 A Answer the questions about the predictions in exercise 3.

1 Which two sentences are about things that are likely?   _____ , _____
2 Which two sentences are about things that are possible? _____ , _____
3 Which two sentences are about things that are unlikely? _____ , _____

B Choose the correct words to complete the rule. Then read the Grammar box.

When we use *probably*, it comes *before / after will* and *before / after won't*.

30

will, *may*, and *might* for predictions ■ jobs **LANGUAGE** **4A**

Grammar *will*, *may*, and *might* for predictions

Predictions that are sure/very likely:	Predictions that are less sure/possible:	Predictions that are very unlikely:
The traffic **will** be very bad tonight.	It **might** rain tomorrow. The train **may** be late.	Chelsea **won't** win the FA cup next year.

Look! We can use *probably* with *will* and *won't*: I'll **probably** fail the exam / I **probably** won't pass the exam.

Go to Grammar practice: *will*, *may*, and *might* for predictions, page 118

5 A ▶ 4.4 **Pronunciation:** *want/won't* Listen and repeat the sentence from the text. Match the words in **bold** with the sounds /a/ and /o/.

In the future, people **won't want** to travel around the world on vacation.

B ▶ 4.5 How do you say the sentences? Pay attention to *want* and *won't*. Listen, check, and repeat.

1 He might **want** to look for a new job.
2 Robots **won't** replace politicians.
3 My boss will probably **want** to travel by boat.
4 In the future, you **won't** have to go to school.

Go to Communication practice: Student A, page 160; Student B, page 168

6 A Work in pairs and look at the topics below. What do you think will happen in the future? Make nine predictions.

Students won't go to school. Computers will probably replace teachers.

50 YEARS FROM NOW...

HOW WILL EDUCATION CHANGE?
1 Students / go to school/college.
2 Computers / replace / teachers.
3 Students / study / different subjects.

HOW WILL TRANSPORTATION BE DIFFERENT?
4 Cars / need / drivers.
5 There / be / more traffic.
6 We / use / electricity as fuel.

WHAT WILL THE HEALTH SYSTEM BE LIKE?
7 There / be / more healthcare jobs.
8 Robots / replace / doctors.
9 We / see the doctor / when we are sick.

B ▶ 4.6 Listen to an expert talking about the topics. What predictions does she make? How sure is she?

7 Did you agree with the expert? Can you think of any other predictions about these topics?

8 In pairs, make predictions about the topics. Say if you agree or disagree with your partner.

- the weather tomorrow
- your country winning the World Cup
- your next English exam
- the town or city where you live
- your trip home tonight
- tomorrow at work/school/college

Personal Best Write predictions about how five different jobs will change in the future.

31

4 SKILLS   READING   skimming a text ■ pronoun referencing

4B I'm so bored!

1 Look at the title and the pictures on page 33. Which jobs can you see? Discuss the questions in pairs.
1. How often do you feel bored?
2. What jobs do you think are boring?
3. Do you think boredom is a bad thing? Why/Why not?
4. What can you do to stop being bored at work?

> **Skill** skimming a text
>
> **When we skim a text, we read it quickly to understand the main ideas.**
> - Look at the title, pictures, and any headings, and predict what the text is about.
> - Read the first sentence in each paragraph carefully. These are "topic sentences" and are usually a summary of what the paragraph is about.
> - Think about the ideas from all the topic sentences to understand the general meaning of the whole text.

2 Read the Skill box. Then read the highlighted topic sentences in the text and check (✓) the best description of the text.
1. Modern technology makes us feel bored more quickly. ☐
2. People can have better ideas after they do boring activities. ☐
3. Boredom in offices is a serious problem for companies. ☐

3 Answer the questions in pairs. Read the text again and check your answers.
1. What do most people do when they are bored?
2. How did the scientists use the plastic cups to test people's creativity?
3. What activity did some people do first to make themselves be bored?
4. Who was more creative in the experiment? What ideas did they have?
5. What does Jack White do to give himself ideas for new songs?
6. What kinds of activities make us more/less creative?

4 Has the text changed your opinion about being bored? Why/Why not?

5 A Look at the extract from the text. Who or what does *They* refer to?

> Some scientists think we're making a mistake. **They** believe that boring activities can be good for us.

B Read the Text builder. Find pronouns 1–8 in the text and say what they refer to.

> **Text builder** pronoun referencing
>
> **We use pronouns and possessive adjectives to avoid repeating nouns:**
> Sharon had **a fantastic idea** yesterday. **It** was really creative.
> **Carlos** always works late. I saw **him** in the office at 8:00 last night.
> **My parents** earn a lot of money, but I think **their** jobs are very boring.

6 A Complete the text with the pronouns in the box. What do the pronouns refer to?

his   it   he   them

> Karl Duncker was a German psychologist. ¹_____ is most famous for developing a way to test creativity. In ²_____ experiment, he gave students a candle, a book of matches, and a box of thumbtacks. He asked ³_____ to stick the candle to a wall and light ⁴_____ without dripping any wax on the table.

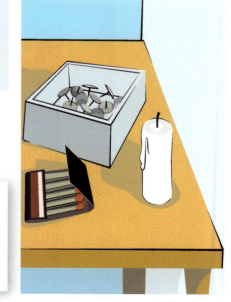

B In pairs, try to solve Duncker's problem. Explain your solution to the class.

skimming a text ■ pronoun referencing   READING   SKILLS   4B

THE TRUTH ABOUT BOREDOM

We all hate being bored, particularly at work. In fact, most of us try hard to avoid [1] **it** and, thanks to modern technology, there are now hundreds of ways to keep ourselves entertained. People watch videos or play games on the way to work, check their phones when they're in boring meetings, and talk with friends or listen to music while they do dull administrative tasks. But some scientists think we're making a mistake. They believe that boring activities can be good for us, and a recent psychology experiment tests this idea.

In 2013, Dr. Sandi Mann and Rebekah Cadman did an experiment to test people's creativity, i.e., how good we are at coming up with new ideas. [2] **Their** idea was to see if boredom had an effect on how creative we are. They gave 140 people some plastic cups and asked [3] **them** to think of different ways to use them. However, half of the people spent 15 minutes doing some very boring activities first. They had to read telephone numbers from a long list and copy [4] **them** on a piece of paper.

The results of the experiment were very interesting. The people who did the boring activities first were much more creative and thought of lots of ideas. Some people suggested wearing the cups as party hats or filling [5] **them** with fruit juice and freezing them to make popsicles. Whereas, the people who didn't do any boring tasks found it hard to think of many ways to use the cups.

Dr. Mann says a little boredom can be positive for us. [6] **She** doesn't think we should be afraid of "doing nothing." Many very successful people do "boring" activities in their free time. For example, rock musician Jack White, repairs furniture. [7] **His** hobby helps him relax and think of ideas for new songs. At work, some successful people do similar things to be more creative, like cleaning out their desk or deleting old e-mails.

However, there are good and bad ways to be bored. You should only do boring activities for a short time. And you should avoid physical activities that make you feel tired, as this can make you less creative. So, if you usually listen to music, read the news, and send messages to friends when you're bored at work, why not try doing less? Make yourself a cup of coffee, organize your paperwork, or look out the window—maybe [8] **it** will change your life … and you can always tell your boss that you're being creative.

Personal Best Write about a time you thought of a creative solution to a problem.

4 LANGUAGE — be going to and present continuous ■ phrases about work

4C The secret boss

1 Look at the two people in the pictures. What is the relationship between them? Read the text and check.

Carla Pine is the managing director of a chain of Italian restaurants. She works in Vancouver and is responsible for twenty restaurants in Canada. Next week, she's visiting two of her restaurants to find out what it's like to be a company employee, but she's going to do it in secret! She's going to dress like a member of the staff but, because people might recognize her, she's going to change her hair color and makeup, and become … Katie Rose.

She's going to Toronto and has a busy few days ahead of her. On Monday and Tuesday, she's working as a kitchen assistant with George Nowak. On Wednesday and Thursday, she's working as a waitress in another restaurant in the city with Lucy Mendez … and on Friday, she's going to tell George and Lucy who she really is!

Carla Pine   Katie Rose

2 Choose the correct options to complete the sentences. Read the text again and check.

1 Carla is visiting *one / two / three* of her restaurants next week.
2 She is going to change her *appearance / opinion / voice* so people don't recognize her.
3 She's going to see what it's like to work as *a hair stylist / a boss / an employee*.
4 On Monday and Tuesday, she's working as a *managing director / waitress / kitchen assistant*.
5 On Wednesday and Thursday, she's working with *Lucy Mendez / George Nowak / Katie Rose*.

3 Answer the questions about the sentences in exercise 2. Then read the Grammar box.

1 Do the sentences refer to the past, the present, or the future? _____
2 Which sentences say *when* and/or *where* she will do things? _____
3 Which use the present continuous? _____ Which use *be going to*? _____

Grammar — be going to and present continuous

Future plans:
I**'m going to take** a training course.
The company **isn't going to open** a new office.

Future arrangements (with a fixed time and place):
He**'s working** in Seattle on Monday.
What **are you doing** this evening?

Look! We can also use *be going to* with arrangements:
He**'s going to** travel to Seattle on Monday.
What **are** you **going to** do this evening?

Go to Grammar practice: *be going to* and present continuous, page 119

4 A ▶ 4.9 **Pronunciation:** *going to* and *want to* Listen to Carla speaking quickly. How are *going to* and *want to* pronounced?

I **want to** find out what it's like to work for my company, so I'm **going to** visit two of my restaurants ... in secret.

B ▶ 4.10 In pairs, say the conversation quickly. Listen, check, and repeat.

A What are you **going to** do tonight?
B I'm **going to** try that new Chinese restaurant. Do you **want to** come?
A I can't. I'm **going to** work late tonight. I'm free tomorrow, if you **want to** get together.
B Yes, that's great. I **want to** hear all your news!

be going to and present continuous ▪ phrases about work   **LANGUAGE 4C**

5 Check (✓) the things you have done from the box below. Tell your partner when and why.

| apply for a job ☐ | take a training course ☐ | get a promotion ☐ | quit a job ☐ | write a résumé ☐ |

When I was a student, I applied for a job as a DJ. I didn't get it.

Go to Vocabulary practice: phrases about work, page 143

6 A ▶ 4.13 Listen to the conversation between Carla, Lucy, and George. Complete the chart.

Name	Problems	Solutions
George Nowak, Head chef	George's kitchen wasn't clean.	
Lucy Mendez, Head waitress		

B Check your answers in pairs.

George's kitchen wasn't clean, so Carla is going to …

7 A In pairs, look at the problems and think of the best way to solve them.

1. Your colleague is going on vacation, so you'll have to use a complicated new computer program at work.
2. Your boss does no work, but he wants you to work on the weekends to finish a project.
3. You want to buy a house, but your salary is the same as when you started work ten years ago!

B Tell the rest of the class your plans.

We're going to take a training course to learn about the new program.

Go to Communication practice: Student A, page 160; Student B, page 168

8 In pairs, ask and answer the question *What are you doing …?* with the future times in the boxes below.

A What are you doing tonight?
B I'm meeting some friends downtown. We're going to have dinner together.

tonight | tomorrow | next weekend | next summer | in two weeks | the day after tomorrow | next year

Personal Best Write about your work plans for the future. 35

4 SKILLS **SPEAKING** telephone language ■ dealing with difficulties

4D Can I leave a message?

1 Look at the reasons for making telephone calls. Can you think of any more?

> call a taxi   speak to a colleague   call in sick to work   ask for technical help
> reserve a table at a restaurant   make an appointment   call a store for information

2 Discuss the questions in pairs.
  1 How often do you call people?
  2 Who do you usually talk to on the phone?
  3 How do you feel when you speak to someone you don't know on the phone?
  4 What problems can you have when you speak in English on the phone?

3 ▶ 4.14 Watch or listen to the first part of *Learning Curve*. Who called these people, and why did they call?

4 ▶ 4.14 Watch or listen again. Are the sentences true (T) or false (F)?
  1 Penny thinks that communication is easier with modern technology. _____
  2 Penny and Ethan have a video conference call with Simon and Kate at 10:00. _____
  3 Ethan makes an appointment with the dentist for 9:50. _____
  4 Mo says it will take ten minutes to fix the Internet connection. _____
  5 Mo says he will bring Penny a telephone to call Simon and Kate. _____

Conversation builder | telephone language

Caller:
Hello, this is …
Could I speak to …?
Can you tell him/her that …?
Could you ask him/her to call me back, please?
Thank you, goodbye.

Person being called:
Good morning, … How can I help you?
Hello, this is … (speaking/calling).
I'm afraid he/she's not available at the moment.
Can I take a message?
I think you have the wrong number.
Thanks/Thank you for calling.

5 A ▶ 4.15 Read the Conversation builder. In pairs, order the conversation from 1–9. Listen and check.

  a ☐ Thanks for calling.
  b ☐ Yes, can you ask her to call Fiona when she can?
  c ☐ Hello, Mo Bensallem speaking.
  d ☐ Yes, of course.
  e ☐ Hello, could I speak to Julia, please?
  f ☐ I'm afraid she's not at her desk at the moment.
  g ☐ Sorry, I don't know. Can I take a message?
  h ☐ Do you know when she will be back?
  i ☐ Thank you, goodbye.

B In pairs, practice saying the conversation. You can change the names and any details.

telephone language ■ dealing with difficulties **SPEAKING** **SKILLS** **4D**

6 ▶ 4.16 Watch or listen to the second part of the show. Does Penny speak to Kate and Simon?

7 ▶ 4.16 Check (✓) the problems Penny has. Watch or listen again and check.
1 She dials the wrong number. ☐
2 Simon forgot about the conference call. ☐
3 Kate doesn't answer the phone in time. ☐
4 Charlotte can't hear Penny very well. ☐
5 Charlotte doesn't understand English well. ☐
6 Penny forgot to leave her number. ☐

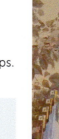
Charlotte

8 ▶ 4.17 Listen and repeat the phrases when you hear the beeps. How do the speakers deal with difficulties?

> **Skill dealing with difficulties**
>
> It is sometimes difficult to understand people when they speak, especially on the telephone.
> • Ask the speaker politely to speak louder or repeat what he/she said.
> • Ask the speaker to spell any difficult words.
> • Repeat what the speaker says to make sure it is correct.
> • Stress any words or phrases you want to check.

9 Read the Skill box. Put the phrases in the correct column.

I'm afraid I didn't catch that.   Did you say …?   And was that … or …?   Sorry, could you speak louder?
Can you spell that for me, please?   Could you speak more slowly, please?   Could you repeat that, please?

You don't hear something	You need to check or confirm specific information

10 A ▶ 4.18 Listen to five conversations and underline the information the speaker wants to check.
1 Sorry, did you say you needed three blue shirts?
2 And you bought the product on June 5, 2010?
3 So your flight is at 5:00 p.m. on Wednesday of next week?
4 Sorry, did you say you wanted to reserve a double room for next week?
5 Was that vegetable soup for table 12?

B In pairs, repeat questions 1–5. Pay attention to the words you stress.

Go to Communication practice: Student A, page 159; Student B, page 167

11 A **PREPARE** In pairs, look at the situations below. Decide which role you will play and think about what you will say.

	Situation 1	Situation 2
Student A	You have arranged to meet with a colleague. Call to cancel the meeting.	You are going on vacation to Acapulco. Make a hotel reservation for your trip.
Student B	Answer the phone. The person the speaker wants to talk to is not in the office. Take a message.	You are a receptionist at a hotel. Write down details of the reservation. It is very noisy, and you can't hear the speaker well.

B **PRACTICE** Sit back to back with your partner so you can't see him/her. Practice the telephone conversation.

C **PERSONAL BEST** Are you more confident at speaking on the telephone in English? How could you improve? Change partners and practice the conversations again.

Personal Best Write down one of the conversations from exercise 11.

37

3 and 4 REVIEW and PRACTICE

Grammar

1 Put a (**X**) by the sentence that is NOT correct.

1. a This hotel is more expensive than Hotel Atlanta.
   b This hotel is the most expensive as Hotel Atlanta.
   c Hotel Atlanta isn't as expensive as this one.
2. a Simon was cutting his finger while cooking.
   b Simon cut his finger while he was cooking.
   c Simon was cooking when he cut his finger.
3. a I don't think he'll win the race.
   b He might not win the race.
   c He might won't win the race.
4. a This phone is the smallest in the store.
   b This phone is smaller than the others.
   c This phone as small as in the store.
5. a It may be hot tomorrow.
   b It will be probably hot tomorrow.
   c It might be hot tomorrow.
6. a What do you do next week?
   b What are you doing next week?
   c What are you going to do next week?
7. a I met Jerry while I was studying in college in 2010.
   b In 2010, while I was studying in college, I met Jerry.
   c I was meeting Jerry in 2010, while I studied in college.
8. a She's not meeting her friend at the theater.
   b She's not going to meet her friend at the theater.
   c She doesn't meet with her friend tonight.

2 Use the words in parentheses to complete the sentences so they mean the same as the first sentence.

1. London isn't as hot as Madrid.
   Madrid _____ London. (hotter)
2. I don't think I will pass the exam.
   I _____ the exam. (probably / pass)
3. Kelly is shorter than Nicki.
   Kelly _____ Nicki. (as / tall)
4. My phone rang while I was cooking dinner.
   _____ my phone rang. (when)
5. He's arriving at 6:00 p.m.
   He's _____ at 6:00 p.m. (going)
6. The store may be closed.
   The store _____ open. (might)
7. I was talking on the phone when I missed my train.
   I missed my train _____. (while)
8. What are you going to do on Saturday?
   What _____ on Saturday? (doing)

3 Choose the correct options to complete the text.

In 2009, Canadian Alex Deans ¹*watched / was watching* a blind person cross the street when he ²*had / was having* a great idea. He realized that he could use sound to help blind people know where things are, like some animals do.

Even though he ³*still studied / was still studying* in high school, he ⁴*found / was finding* time to develop his idea. Four years later, he finished work on the i-Aid, a device that makes it ⁵*easier / easiest* for blind people to move around objects.

In 2013, he won an award for the ⁶*better / best* invention in Canada and gained a great deal of interest from tech companies. In fact, the Canadian Institute for the Blind was very impressed. The blind people at the institute immediately started testing the device, and the results were very positive.

Deans will ⁷*might / probably* have to wait a couple of years to see the i-Aid in stores, but he is just as ⁸*busy / busier* as before. Right now, he ⁹*is studying / going to study* engineering in college, and whichever project he's working on, it ¹⁰*will / may* definitely be just as exciting as the i-Aid.

Vocabulary

1 Match the words in the box with the definitions.

souvenir   modern   sunbathe   resort
famous   expensive   crowded   pack

1. to put things in a bag for a trip _____
2. something that reminds you of a vacation _____
3. known and recognized by many people _____
4. to relax in the sun _____
5. full of people _____
6. up to date _____
7. costing a lot of money _____
8. an area where tourists stay and do activities _____

REVIEW and PRACTICE **3** and **4**

2 Circle the word that is different. Explain your answer.

1	lively	busy	quiet	quickly
2	a hotel	a table	a museum	a double room
3	surgeon	model	firefighter	police officer
4	résumé	raise	salary	promotion
5	scientist	tour guide	travel agent	flight attendant
6	ad	apply	career	degree
7	lively	polluted	crowded	ugly
8	hire	abroad	eat out	pack

3 Complete the sentences with the words in the box.

> tour guide   movie director   fashion designer
> flight attendant   soccer coach   news reporter

1 He's my favorite _____ , but his clothes are really uncomfortable. You can't wear them for long.

2 The _____ was happy when the team won. It was a difficult game, though. They only won by one goal.

3 The _____ will meet you in the main square. It's very busy, so look for this sign.

4 My sister is a _____ . She flew to 50 different foreign countries last year.

5 My cousin is a _____ . He knows lots of famous actors.

6 I work as a _____ for my city's radio station. I talk about interesting events in the area.

4 Complete the conversation with the verbs in the box.

> write   get   go (x2)   start   see   book
> visit   quit   apply

Omar   Did you [1]_____ the job ad in yesterday's newspaper?

Nuria   No, I didn't.

Omar   Royal Airlines is looking for new flight attendants. You said you wanted to [2]_____ your job.

Nuria   Do you think I should [3]_____ for the job?

Omar   Yes, it's perfect for you! Didn't you want to [4]_____ abroad more often?

Nuria   Yes, but on vacation. I don't think you have much time to [5]_____ sightseeing or [6]_____ local attractions.

Omar   Not when you're working, but you'll probably get a discount when you [7]_____ flights, so you can travel more on vacation!

Nuria   Hmm, maybe. What's the salary?

Omar   It's fairly low when you [8]_____ work, but you might [9]_____ a pay raise after a year or two. I'll help you [10]_____ a résumé, if you want.

Nuria   OK, I'll do it!

Personal Best

Lesson 3A
Write two sentences about your friends using (not) as … as.

Lesson 4A
Write two predictions about next year.

Lesson 3A
Write two sentences about where you live using comparatives and superlatives.

Lesson 4B
Name three pronouns and three possessive adjectives.

Lesson 3B
Name five things you usually do on vacation.

Lesson 4C
Name three things an employee usually does.

Lesson 3C
Write what you were doing at this time yesterday.

Lesson 4C
Think of three plans or arrangements you have for tomorrow.

Lesson 3C
Write a sentence using the simple past and the past continuous.

Lesson 4D
Give three expressions you can use if someone calls you on the telephone.

Lesson 3D
Describe three things you did yesterday using adverbs of manner.

Lesson 4D
Give three expressions you can use when you have problems understanding something.

UNIT 5 Mind and body

LANGUAGE should/shouldn't ■ health and medicine

5A Should I see a doctor?

1 Match the speech bubbles with the pictures.

1 I have a headache.
2 I cut my finger.
3 I'm stressed.
4 I have the flu.
5 I have a cough.

Go to Vocabulary practice: health and medicine, page 144

2 Look at the title and the pictures in the text. In pairs, try to match the strange health tips with the problems in exercise 1. Read the text quickly and check.

Five strange health tips that you should know about

The Internet is full of websites that offer health tips, some serious and some strange. Here are our top five tips from the web … do they work? You can decide on that!

Do you have a temperature or the flu? Then you should put some onion in your socks and wear them at night. You'll feel much better the next morning. Remember though, you shouldn't eat the onion afterward!	You're chopping vegetables in the kitchen and you cut your thumb. What should you do? Put a little black pepper on the cut, of course! It stops the bleeding and helps the cut get better. But you should only do this for small cuts. For anything serious, you should see a doctor.	Do you have regular headaches? Then you should always have an apple nearby. Some studies have found that the smell of green apples can help with headaches and can also make you feel less anxious.	Are you stressed? You should call your mom. A study by the University of Wisconsin showed that people who had more contact with their mother had lower levels of stress. So you shouldn't delay—call her today!	If you have a cough that won't go away, then you should eat some chocolate. Scientists say that chocolate contains a chemical that is better at stopping coughs than many cough medicines. So you shouldn't go to a pharmacy—go to a candy store.

3 Discuss the questions in pairs.

1 Would you try any of the tips? Why/Why not?
2 Do you know any other strange health tips?
3 Do you ever use the Internet to look for health advice?
4 What are the advantages and disadvantages of using the Internet for this?

should/shouldn't ■ health and medicine   LANGUAGE 5A

4 A Look at the question and sentence from the text. Check (✓) the correct meaning.
Are you stressed? You should call your mom.
1 It's necessary to call your mom if you are stressed. ☐
2 It's a good idea to call your mom if you are stressed. ☐
3 It's a bad idea to call your mom if you are stressed. ☐

B Complete the sentences with the words in the box. Check your answers in the text. Then read the Grammar box.

| do   go   put   should (x2)   shouldn't |

1 What _____ you _____ ?
2 You _____ _____ some onion in your socks.
3 You _____ _____ to a pharmacy.

Grammar should/shouldn't

Ask for advice: What **should** I do?
Say something is a good idea: You **should** see a doctor.   I think you **should** get help.
Say something is a bad idea: You **shouldn't** trust tips on the Internet.   I don't think you **should** go to work.

Go to Grammar practice: should/shouldn't, page 120

5 A ▶ 5.3 **Pronunciation:** *should/shouldn't* How do you say *should* and *shouldn't*? Listen to the sentences and check.
1 What should we do?
2 Why shouldn't I speak to him?
3 I think you should talk to an expert.
4 You shouldn't believe him.

B ▶ 5.3 Underline the stressed words in each sentence. Listen, check, and repeat.

6 A Complete the conversation with *should* and *shouldn't* to give health advice.

Paul I'm really stressed. I can't sleep. What ¹_____ I do?
Doctor Well, I don't think you ²_____ work so many hours, and you ³_____ go to bed so late. You ⁴_____ try to get more exercise. That will help you to sleep better.
Paul ⁵_____ I drink less coffee?
Doctor Yes, you ⁶_____ ! And you ⁷_____ drink more water, too.
Paul OK, thank you.
Doctor If that doesn't help, you ⁸_____ come to see me again.

B ▶ 5.4 Listen and check. Repeat the conversation in pairs.

Go to Communication practice: Student A, page 161; Student B, page 169

7 A Discuss these situations in pairs. What advice would you give?

I forgot my friend's birthday and now she's really angry with me. What do you think I should do?
Sara

My roommate is really messy. The kitchen is always dirty after he cooks, and he takes my food from the refrigerator without asking. I don't know what to do!
Enrique

My boss wants me to go to a work conference in New York. The only problem is that it's the same date as my wedding anniversary. What should I tell my wife?
Julio

B Tell the rest of the class your advice. Who had the best ideas?

Personal Best Think of a common health problem and write down five examples of advice.   41

5 SKILLS LISTENING listening in detail ■ linking consonants and vowels ■ verb collocations

5B Modern life is stressful

1 Look at the pictures. In pairs, order them from 1 (most stressful) to 5 (least stressful).

a interviews

b presentations

c exams

d traffic

e moving

2 Read the text. Complete the tips with *do*, *make*, *have*, or *take*.

The best ways to deal with stress

Over 60% of adults say their lives are too stressful. So if you´re stressed right now, you should stop for a minute and read our tips—they might be very helpful!

1 First, _____ **a deep breath** and give yourself time to think.
2 Then _____ **a list** of everything you have to do.
3 Next, _____ **a decision** about what you can realistically do today.
4 Remember to _____ **a break** every two or three hours.
5 You should _____ **something** that makes you feel happy.
6 Try to _____ **a talk** with friends and family about the situation.
7 And finally, _____ **your best** to eat well, exercise, and get at least eight hours' sleep.

Go to Vocabulary practice: collocations with *do*, *make*, *have*, and *take*, page 145

3 Ask and answer the questions in pairs.

1 Do you think your life is stressful? Why/Why not?
2 What things make you feel stressed?
3 Do you think the tips are useful? Why/Why not?
4 Can you think of any other ways to deal with stress?

Skill listening in detail

It is often important to understand what someone says in detail.
- Read the questions carefully and think about the possible answers.
- Listen carefully to everything the speaker says before you answer the question.
- Pay attention to how the things the speaker says relate to each other.
- Be careful in case the speaker changes his/her mind or corrects himself/herself.

4 A ▶ 5.6 Read the Skill box. Watch or listen to the first part of *Learning Curve*. Choose the correct options to answer the questions.

1 How does Simon deal with stress?
  a He makes a list of jobs.   b He walks around.   c He talks to his brother.
2 How many people in the U.S. suffer from stress every day?
  a 77% of citizens   b 400,000 people   c only a small number of people
3 What do some scientists say about a small amount of stress?
  a It can make us sick.   b It makes us feel bored.   c It can help us work better.

B ▶ 5.6 Compare your answers in pairs. Watch or listen again and check.

42

listening in detail ■ linking consonants and vowels ■ verb collocations   **LISTENING**   SKILLS   **5B**

5 A ▶5.7   Watch or listen to the second part of the show. Match the names of the speakers with the tips for dealing with stress.

1 running _____   2 speaking to family _____   3 doing yoga _____

B ▶5.7   Watch or listen again. Are the sentences true (T) or false (F)?

1 Taylor helps people who suffer from stress. ____
2 She thinks complaining about stress can help. ____
3 Edward's boss makes him feel stressed at work. ____
4 He listens to music while he's running. ____
5 Maurice had a stressful job. ____
6 He uses his phone to deal with stress. ____

6 Discuss the questions in pairs.

1 Do you think life today is more stressful than 50 years ago? Why/Why not?
2 Do you think a little stress can be good for us? Why/Why not?

> **Listening builder**   **linking consonants and vowels**
>
> When a word ends in a consonant sound and the next word begins with a vowel sound, we often link the words together:
> *Kate likes to take‿a break once‿an‿hour‿and walk‿around.*

7 ▶5.8   Read the Listening builder. Look at the sentences from the program and mark where you think the words link. Listen, check, and repeat.

1 After a long day I take a hot shower.
2 Kate is on the street doing an interview.
3 After work, I run about five miles a day.
4 And we talk on the phone every day.

8 ▶5.9   Listen and complete the conversation.

Edward   I don't think I can _____ more.
Lara   What's wrong, Edward? Tell _____.
Edward   I _____ work to do … and no time!
Lara   I can help. Let's _____ your jobs for today.

9 Discuss the questions in pairs.

1 What do you think the biggest cause of stress is for most people?
2 What do you think the most stressful stage of our lives is?
3 Think of three stressful jobs. Are there any advantages to these jobs?
4 Think of three low-stress jobs. What kind of job would you prefer? Why?

Personal Best   Write your own list of five tips to beat stress.

5 LANGUAGE   first conditional ■ emotions and feelings

5C How to be happy

1 A How do you think the woman is feeling? Match the adjectives in the box with the pictures.

| calm   delighted   upset   cheerful   nervous |

a  b   c  d   e

B In pairs, think of situations that make people feel these emotions.
An exam can make you feel nervous.

Go to Vocabulary practice: emotions and feelings, page 146

2 A Do you think money makes people happy? Why/Why not?

B Read the text. Check (✓) the sentence that best summarizes the main idea.

1 People with a lot of money often feel miserable. ☐
2 If people have less money, they often feel envious of others. ☐
3 Spending money on other people can make you feel good. ☐

CAN MONEY BUY YOU HAPPINESS?

The Beatles may have been right when they sang "money can't buy me love" but, according to a new study, it can buy you happiness—if you spend it in the right way. Many people think that they'll be happier if they earn more money. But Dr. Michael Norton from Harvard Business School believes that it's not about how much money you make, but about how you spend it.

Dr. Norton tried an experiment with people in different countries. At the start of the experiment, he asked people how happy they were. Then he gave them an envelope with some money and instructions on how to spend it. Some people had to spend the money on themselves, and others were told to spend it on someone else. At the end of the experiment, they measured how happy the people felt again.

The results show that if you spend money on other people, you'll feel happier. And if you only spend money on yourself, you won't feel any different. So the next time you want to buy a new TV or some new clothes, ask yourself, "If I buy this, will it make me happier?" According to Dr. Norton, we should think less about ourselves and more about others because, if we do that, we'll feel much better!

3 A Complete the sentence. Check your answers in the text.

If you _____ money on other people, you _____ feel happier.
          A   B

B Answer the questions about the two parts of the sentence: A and B. Then read the Grammar box.

1 Which part of the sentence is a possible future action? ____ What tense is the verb? _____
2 Which part of the sentence is the result of that action? ____ What tense is the verb? _____
3 Can we rewrite the sentence so that part B comes first and part A comes second? _____

📖 Grammar   first conditional

Possible future action:
If it **rains** tomorrow,
If the train **doesn't arrive**,
If she **fails** the exam,

Result of action:
Laura **won't go** to the beach.
I'll be late for the meeting.
will she **have** to do it again?

Look! We can change the order of the clauses: *Laura won't go to the beach if it rains tomorrow.*

Go to Grammar practice: first conditional, page 121

first conditional ■ emotions and feelings   LANGUAGE 5C

4 A ▶ 5.12 Listen to the conversation. Why doesn't Sam accept the movie ticket? Do you think this is a good reason?

B Complete Sam's reason. Listen again and check.

If I ¹_____ to the movies, we ²_____ a scary movie. And if I ³_____ a scary movie, I ⁴_____ nervous. And if I ⁵_____ nervous, I ⁶_____ well tonight. And if I ⁷_____ well, I ⁸_____ late for work. And if I ⁹_____ late for work, my boss ¹⁰_____ angry. And if my boss ¹¹_____ angry, I ¹²_____ a pay raise. And if I ¹³_____ a pay raise, I ¹⁴_____ on vacation. And if I ¹⁵_____ on vacation, I ¹⁶_____ miserable. So, no thank you!

5 A ▶ 5.13 **Pronunciation:** *'ll contraction* How do you say *'ll*? Listen, check, and repeat.

I'll   you'll   he'll   she'll   it'll   we'll   they'll

B ▶ 5.14 Match the two columns to make sentences. In pairs, say the sentences. Pay attention to the *'ll* sound. Listen, check, and repeat.

1 I'll be really envious
2 You'll miss your flight
3 If you give her your phone number,
4 If you can fix the computer now,
5 If she fails her exam,
6 They'll get a taxi

a she'll call you later.
b if your boss sends you to Jamaica.
c she'll be really upset.
d if you can't take them to the station.
e if you don't leave now.
f it'll be very helpful.

Go to Communication practice: Student A, page 161; Student B, page 169

6 A Take the quiz in pairs. Write down your partner's answers.

B Go to page 174 and look at the results. Do you agree with them? Why/Why not?

How happy are you?

1 If I wake up very early tomorrow morning, …
 a I'll be miserable all day.
 b I'll try to go back to sleep.
 c I'll get up and make a big breakfast.
 d I might go running or work out at the gym.

2 If my best friend buys a new laptop, …
 a I might feel a little envious.
 b I'll buy an even better one.
 c I might look for a new one, too.
 d I'll be delighted for him/her.

3 If I find some money on the street next week, …
 a I'll put it in my bank account.
 b I'll buy myself some new clothes.
 c I'll give it to the police.
 d I'll donate it to charity.

4 If my boss asks to speak to me, …
 a I'll think he/she wants to fire me.
 b I'll probably feel very nervous.
 c I'll be calm and find out what he/she wants.
 d I'll think I'm going to get a promotion.

5 If my parents give me a present that I don't really want, …
 a I'll ask for the receipt and exchange it for something I like.
 b I'll thank them, but say I don't want the present.
 c I'll say thanks, but use it as a present for someone else.
 d I'll tell them I love it and try to use it in some way.

7 A In pairs, complete the sentences.
1 If I make a lot of money, …
2 If I get a headache later, …
3 I won't believe it if …
4 I'll be delighted if …
5 If I don't come to class next week, …
6 I'll have a big party if …

B Tell the class what your partner said.

Personal Best Write twelve first conditional sentences with all the emotions and feelings words from the Vocabulary practice on p. 146.

45

5 SKILLS WRITING writing an informal e-mail ▪ modifiers

5D I need your advice

1 In pairs, order the work problems from 1 (most serious) to 6 (least serious).

> lazy colleagues   mean boss
> boring work   too many working hours
> low salary   long trip to work

2 Look at the picture of Tom, who works at a busy health club. Guess the answers to the questions in pairs.
1 How is he feeling?
2 What problems does he have at work?

3 Read the e-mail and check your answers to exercise 2.

1 _____ Catching up

2 _____ Hi Duncan,

3 _____ How's it going? Hope you're well. I'm still working at the health club, but I'm not very happy. That's why I'm writing. I wanted to ask you for some advice.

4 _____ One of my colleagues, Sebastian, is really lazy, and he's not very nice to me, either. Whenever there's a problem, our manager always blames me! I also think his friends use the gym without paying. What do you think I should do? If I tell the manager, it might cause even more problems with Sebastian!

5 _____ Anyway, I saw an ad for a job at a new gym the other day. If I start work there, the salary will be lower, but it's a large chain, so there might be more opportunities in the future. Do you think I should apply? Do you feel like getting together for coffee some time this week so we can talk about it? Let me know when you're free.

6 _____ See you later,
Tom

4 Label the sections of the e-mail with the words in the box.

> details   ending   subject   reason for writing   greeting   request for response

🔧 Skill writing an informal e-mail

We write informal e-mails to people we know well, such as friends, family, and colleagues.
- Structure the e-mail with a subject, greeting, reason for writing, details, request for a response, and an ending.
- Use contractions like *I'm, he's,* and *don't.*
- Use informal words and phrases like *Hi, How's it going?,* and *anyway.*

5 Read the Skill box. Find the informal words and phrases in the e-mail for phrases 1–6.
1 Hello _____
2 How are you? _____
3 On another subject … _____
4 Would you like to … _____
5 Please tell me _____
6 Goodbye _____

writing an informal e-mail ■ modifiers **WRITING** SKILLS **5D**

6 Discuss the questions in pairs.
1 Do you ever have problems similar to Tom's?
2 Who do you talk to about problems at work?
3 What should Tom do about Sebastian?
4 What should Tom do about the job ad?

7 Read Duncan's reply. Do you agree with him? Why/Why not?

RE: Catching up

Hi Tom,
Good to hear from you! I'm OK, thanks, but I was **very** sorry to hear your news about work. Everyone has colleagues who are **a little** lazy like Sebastian, but the problem with his friends using the gym is serious. I think you should speak to him first. Explain that it's like stealing money from the company, and if he doesn't stop, you'll have to tell the manager. I know she's **not very** nice, but it's **really** important to tell her.
You also mentioned applying for another job. I think it's an **extremely** good idea. If you get the job, you can ask for the same salary as you earn now, and you might get a promotion **pretty** quickly in the future.
I'd love to get together. I'll be in town next Thursday evening. Let me know where and when you want to meet.

All the best,
Duncan

---

8 A Look at the modifiers in **bold** in Duncan's e-mail and complete the rules.
1 Modifiers make adjectives and adverbs *stronger / weaker / both stronger and weaker*.
2 Modifiers come *before / after* adjectives and adverbs.

B Put the words in **bold** in the correct places in the diagram.

1 extremely 2 _____ _fairly_ 5 _____ _not at all_
3 _____ 4 _____ 6 _____

Text builder | **modifiers**

We use modifiers to make adjectives and adverbs stronger or weaker:
Be careful, the soup is **extremely** hot.
She was driving **very** fast when the accident happened.
I'm **a little** nervous about the exam next week.

Look! We usually use *a little* with negative adjectives:
She's **a little** upset today NOT ~~She's a little cheerful today~~.

---

9 Read the Text builder. Complete the sentences with a modifier and an adjective. Compare your answers in pairs.
1 Most of my friends are ...
2 Learning English is ...
3 Today, I'm feeling ...
4 My job is ...
5 The weather is ...
6 Eating out is ...

10 A PREPARE Choose one of the problems.
• Your parents want you to study medicine, but you don't want to. You would prefer to study music.
• You want to get in shape, but you only have a few hours a week free and don't have very much money.
• Your boss gives you too much work. You are worried that if you refuse to do it, you might lose your job.

B PRACTICE Write an e-mail to a friend asking for advice about the problem.

C PERSONAL BEST Exchange e-mails with a partner. Underline five things that you think are very good.

Personal Best | Write a reply to your partner's e-mail. Try to use different modifiers.

UNIT 6 Risks and experiences

LANGUAGE present perfect with *ever* and *never* ■ phrasal verbs

6A Try something new!

1 Look at the pictures. Ask and answer the questions in pairs.
1 Which activities are the most difficult, in your opinion?
2 Which activities would you like to try? Why/Why not?
3 What stopped you from doing these activities in the past?

learn to play an instrument

climb a mountain | ride your bike to work | read a book in a foreign language | do an extreme sport

2 Read the text. Which activities from exercise 1 has Matt Cutts done?

The 30-day Challenge

Have you ever wanted to try something new? Perhaps you've wanted to take up a new hobby or learn a new skill. What stopped you? Not enough time? The fear of failure? Was it difficult to change your routine?

Matt Cutts is an American software engineer. A few years ago, he was bored with his life. That's when he decided to try the 30-day challenge. The idea is simple. You think of something you haven't done before, but you've always wanted to do, and you try it for 30 days. He started with small challenges, such as walking more, riding his bike to work, and giving up sugar for a month. Gradually, his challenges became bigger and more difficult. Now, Matt has written a novel, he's taught himself to play the ukulele, and he's even climbed Mount Kilimanjaro!
Trying something new can be kind of terrifying, but doing it for just 30 days doesn't seem so hard. At the end of the month, you can stop … or who knows? You might decide to go on with your new activity. For example, Matt gave up TV and did other things like reading books, instead. After 30 days, the first thing he did was turn on the TV. However, he found that he watched less TV than before because he enjoyed doing the other things, too.
Matt says that the challenges have made his life much more interesting. He's also become more confident. So, what about you? Is there something you've always wanted to do? What are you waiting for? **Try it for 30 days!**

3 Answer the questions in pairs.
1 Why did Matt start doing 30-day challenges?
2 Why is it easier to try something for 30 days?
3 How have the challenges helped Matt?
4 What challenge would you do for 30 days?

4 Choose the correct words to complete the sentences. Check your answers in the text.
1 Maybe you've wanted to **take** up / over / in a new hobby or learn a new skill.
2 You might decide to **go** over / in / on with your new activity.
3 Matt **gave** under / up / above TV and did other things like reading books, instead.
4 After 30 days, the first thing he did was **turn** on / in / around the TV.

Go to Vocabulary practice: phrasal verbs, page 145

48

present perfect with *ever* and *never* ■ phrasal verbs **LANGUAGE** — **6A**

5 **A** Complete the sentences about Matt from the text. Check your answers in the text.

1 A few years ago, he _____ bored with his life. 2 Matt has _____ a novel.

B Answer the questions about sentences 1 and 2 in exercise 5A.

1 Which sentence is about an event at a particular time in the past? ____
What is the tense? *simple past / present perfect*
2 Which sentence is about a general experience in Matt's life? ____
What is the tense? *simple past / present perfect*
3 How do we form the present perfect tense? the verb _____ + past participle

6 Underline a present perfect question and an example of the present perfect negative in the text.
Then read the Grammar box.

> 📖 **Grammar** | **present perfect with *ever* and *never***
>
> **Experiences in your life:**
> ***Have*** you **ever eaten** Japanese food? I **'ve been** to Australia, but I **'ve never seen** a kangaroo.
> She **hasn't seen** the new Star Wars movie.
>
> **Look!** We use the simple past to talk about **when** an event happened and to give more details:
> *I've been to the U.S. I **went** to California in 2015. It **was** great!*

Personal Best

Go to Grammar practice: present perfect with *ever* and *never*, page 122

7 ▶ 6.4 **Pronunciation:** irregular past participles Listen and repeat the words. Pay attention to
the /ən/ sound in the *-en* endings.

brok**en**   chos**en**   driv**en**   eat**en**   fall**en**   forgot**ten**   giv**en**   spok**en**   tak**en**   writt**en**

8 **A** ▶ 6.5 Practice saying the questions. Listen, check, and repeat.

1 Have you ever writt**en** a poem?   4 Have you ever brok**en** your arm or leg?
2 Have you ever eat**en** Japanese food?   5 Have you ever forgot**ten** an important birthday?
3 Have you ever driv**en** a fast car?   6 Have you ever fall**en** asleep in class or at work?

B Ask and answer the questions in pairs. If you answer *Yes, I have*, give more information in the
simple past.

A *Have you ever written a poem?*   **B** *Yes, I have. I had to write a poem when I was at school.*

Go to Communication practice: Student A, page 161; Student B, page 169

9 **A** ▶ 6.6 Complete the text with the present perfect form of the verbs in the box. Listen and check.

study   give up   write   win   work   be

DID YOU KNOW ...?

Natalie Portman is a world-famous actress.
You probably know that she [1]_____ an
Oscar, but here are some facts you might
not know.

⭐ She [2]_____ with Britney Spears.
⭐ She [3]_____ two scientific papers that
  [4]_____ published.
⭐ She [5]_____ Japanese, German, and Arabic.
⭐ She [6]_____ watching TV.

B ▶ 6.6 Listen again. Are the sentences true (T) or false (F)?

1 Natalie was the main character in a musical when she was 10 years old. ____
2 She studied psychology at Harvard University. ____
3 She started learning languages when she was a child. ____
4 She never watches any TV shows. ____

10 **A** Write down some of your experiences that not many people know about.

B In pairs, talk about your experiences and give more information.

Personal Best Write ten sentences about yourself using the phrasal verbs in the Vocabulary practice. 49

6 SKILLS READING guessing the meaning of words from context ■ linkers to add extra information

6B An amazing story

1 Look at the pictures on page 51. Discuss the questions in pairs.
1 Have you seen the movie *127 Hours*?
2 If you have seen it, what is it about? If you haven't, can you guess what happens in it?
3 Have you ever tried rock climbing?
4 What problems could you have doing this activity?

2 Read the safety advice and guess which three mistakes Aron made. Read the text quickly and check your answers.

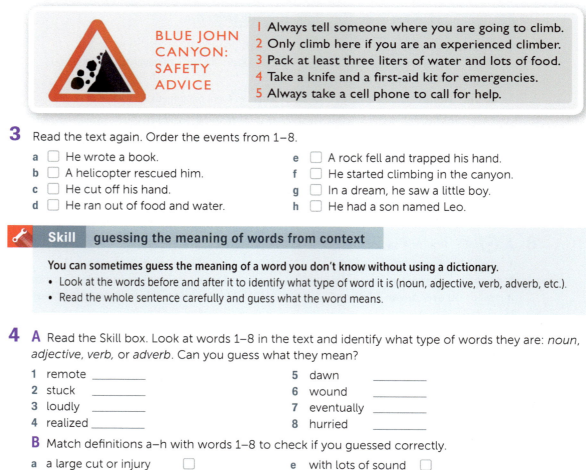

BLUE JOHN CANYON: SAFETY ADVICE
1 Always tell someone where you are going to climb.
2 Only climb here if you are an experienced climber.
3 Pack at least three liters of water and lots of food.
4 Take a knife and a first-aid kit for emergencies.
5 Always take a cell phone to call for help.

3 Read the text again. Order the events from 1–8.
a ☐ He wrote a book.
b ☐ A helicopter rescued him.
c ☐ He cut off his hand.
d ☐ He ran out of food and water.
e ☐ A rock fell and trapped his hand.
f ☐ He started climbing in the canyon.
g ☐ In a dream, he saw a little boy.
h ☐ He had a son named Leo.

Skill guessing the meaning of words from context

You can sometimes guess the meaning of a word you don't know without using a dictionary.
• Look at the words before and after it to identify what type of word it is (noun, adjective, verb, adverb, etc.).
• Read the whole sentence carefully and guess what the word means.

4 A Read the Skill box. Look at words 1–8 in the text and identify what type of words they are: *noun, adjective, verb,* or *adverb*. Can you guess what they mean?

1 remote _____
2 stuck _____
3 loudly _____
4 realized _____
5 dawn _____
6 wound _____
7 eventually _____
8 hurried _____

B Match definitions a–h with words 1–8 to check if you guessed correctly.
a a large cut or injury ☐
b far away ☐
c the first light of the day ☐
d moved quickly ☐
e with lots of sound ☐
f after some time ☐
g understood a fact ☐
h unable to move ☐

Text builder linkers to add extra information

We use the linkers *and, also, as well,* and *too* to add extra information:
• *and* comes between two phrases: *It's a very beautiful place, and it's very remote.*
• *also* comes before the main verb: *He also gives talks about his adventure.*
• *as well* and *too* come at the end of a phrase: *… he was alone, as well. … he pushed with his feet, too.*

5 Read the Text builder. Discuss the questions in pairs and add extra information with the linkers.

A *I think Aron was stupid because he didn't take a phone.*
B *Yes, but he was brave, as well.*

1 How would you describe Aron?
2 What would you do in Aron's situation?
3 What advice do you think he gives in his talks?
4 What would you pack on a trip to the desert?

ARON RALSTON'S AMAZING STORY

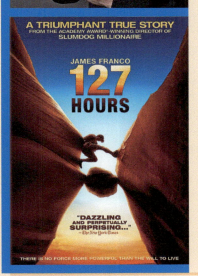

Aron Ralston is an experienced climber, but one day in 2003, he forgot a few basic rules, and a day in the desert turned into a nightmare that lasted nearly a week. That particular day, he went rock climbing in Blue John Canyon in Utah, U.S. It's a very beautiful place and it's very [1]**remote**, a long drive from the nearest town. The problems began when he didn't tell anyone where he was going, so nobody knew he was there.

A few hours later, he was climbing in the canyon when suddenly a big rock fell and trapped his right hand against the canyon wall. Trying not to panic, he pulled with his left arm and pushed with his feet, too, but he couldn't move the rock even one centimeter. He was [2]**stuck** and alone, as well.

He had left his phone in his car, so he couldn't call for help. He tried shouting [3]**loudly**, but there was nobody to hear him. In his bag, there was a small bottle of water, two burritos and some chocolate—enough food for a short walk. Waiting for help day after day, he ate his food and drank the water slowly, but no help came. He [4]**realized** he was probably going to die and recorded video messages for his family on a camera.

After five days, all of his food and water were gone. That night, he had a strange dream and saw a small boy who was his future son. He woke up at [5]**dawn** the following morning and he knew what he had to do. The only way to escape was to cut off his hand.

First, he broke his arm, and then he used a small knife to remove his hand. It took an hour and was extremely painful. He used a small first-aid kit on the [6]**wound**, but he was losing a lot of blood. He managed to climb down the canyon and walked slowly toward his car. [7]**Eventually**, he met a Dutch family who gave him food and [8]**hurried** to find help. Soon after, a helicopter arrived to rescue him.

Aron wrote a book about his experience, and director Danny Boyle made the story into a movie. Seven years after the accident, Aron had a son named Leo, and today he still goes climbing. He also gives talks about his adventure to help other people.

6 LANGUAGE second conditional ■ the natural world

6C Into the wild

1 Read the text and answer the questions in pairs.

1 Would you like to have Gemma's job?
2 What are the best and worst things about it?
3 Do you think you could survive in the wild?
4 Which photo do you prefer? Why?

Gemma Tang is a professional photographer and survival specialist. She grew up in Guangzhou, China, but has spent years traveling around the world, taking amazing photos of wildlife and spectacular landscapes. She is currently living in Cuzco, Peru where she runs survival courses in the Amazon rainforest. A new exhibit of her photos just opened in London. Here are two of the best.

2 Match the words in the box with parts of the landscapes.

cliff   waves   peak   sunset   waterfall   rocks

1 _____ 2 _____ 3 _____ 4 _____ 5 _____ 6 _____

Go to Vocabulary practice: the natural world, page 147

3 A ▶ 6.8 In pairs, do the survival quiz. Listen to Gemma and check your answers.

B Look at page 174 and read the results. Do you agree? Why/Why not?

SURVIVAL QUIZ

1 If I were in the mountains and saw a bear outside its cave, …
   a I'd run away as fast as possible.
   b I'd climb the nearest tree.
   c I'd take a photo. What an opportunity!

2 If I were on a hike in the rainforest and ran out of food, …
   a I'd eat a small animal, like a tarantula.
   b I'd find some plants and eat them.
   c I wouldn't eat anything.

3 If I were swimming in the ocean and saw a shark in the water, …
   a I'd scream and swim in the opposite direction.
   b I'd move towards the shark and kick it in the nose.
   c I'd try to swim quickly and quietly away.

4 If I were hiking and needed to drink some water, …
   a I'd drink the water from a river or lake.
   b I'd find a stream to get water.
   c I wouldn't drink any water.

4 ▶ 6.8 Listen again and answer the questions.

1 Why should you climb up high in a tree? _____
2 What do tarantulas taste like? _____
3 What percentage of sharks don't attack humans? _____
4 What can river water contain? _____

52

second conditional ■ the natural world **LANGUAGE 6C**

5 **A** ▶ 6.9 Match the two parts to make sentences from the audio. Listen and check.
1 If you ran,   a I wouldn't take a photo.
2 If I were in this situation,   b would you look for a stream?
3 If you needed water,   c the bear would follow you.

B Answer the questions. Then read the Grammar box.
1 Which tense do we use after *if*?   _____
2 Which auxiliary verb do we use with the base form in the second part of the sentence?   _____
3 Are these situations impossible or unlikely?   _____
4 What do you notice about the past tense of *be* in sentence 2?   _____

Grammar   second conditional

Impossible or very unlikely situations:
If I **saw** a bear in the mountains, I**'d run**.
If he **ran out** of food in the rainforest, he **wouldn't eat** anything.
What **would** you **do if** you **saw** a shark in the ocean?

Look! We can use **were** instead of **was** in the second conditional:
I wouldn't drink the river water if I **were** you.

Go to Grammar practice: second conditional, page 123

6 **A** ▶ 6.11 **Pronunciation: sentence stress** Listen to the sentences from conversations 1–3. Underline the stressed words.
1 If I saw a bear, I'd run.
2 If you ate a poisonous one, it would make you sick.
3 I wouldn't eat a spider if it were the last food on earth.
4 I wouldn't survive five minutes in the wild!

B Practice saying the sentences in pairs.

7 In pairs, look at the situations and make sentences about what you would and wouldn't do. Pay attention to the sentence stress.

If I found a wallet on the street, I wouldn't spend the money. I'd try to find the owner.

1 If I found a wallet on the street, ...	2 If I accidentally hit a parked car with my car, ...	3 If I was invited to a costume party, ...

a give it to the police	a leave my phone number	a make an excuse and not go
b spend the money	b drive away	b make an amazing costume
c try to find the owner	c wait for the owner to return	c wear a silly hat

Go to Communication practice: Student A, page 161; Student B, page 169

8 Discuss the questions in pairs.
What would you do if ...
1 you didn't have to work?
2 a salesperson gave you too much change?
3 you saw a colleague stealing from work?
4 you found a spider in the bathtub?
5 your boss offered you a job in New York?
6 your parents forgot your birthday?
7 you couldn't use the Internet for a week?
8 you met a famous person in the supermarket?

Personal Best Write a paragraph about what you would do if you won a competition to go anywhere in the world.

6 SKILLS SPEAKING agreeing and disagreeing ■ taking turns

6D Would you take the risk?

1 A Are you a risk-taker? In pairs, ask and answer the questions to find out.

B Look at the results on page 174. Do you agree? Why/Why not?

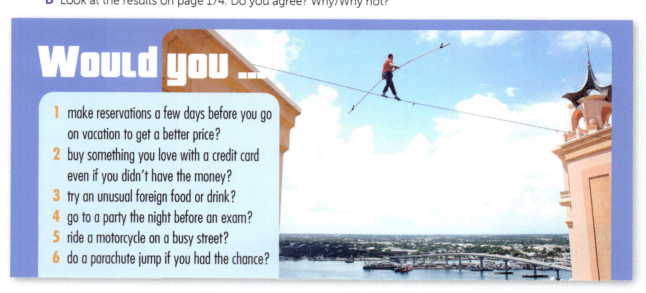

Would you …
1. make reservations a few days before you go on vacation to get a better price?
2. buy something you love with a credit card even if you didn't have the money?
3. try an unusual foreign food or drink?
4. go to a party the night before an exam?
5. ride a motorcycle on a busy street?
6. do a parachute jump if you had the chance?

2 ▶ 6.12 Watch or listen to the first part of *Learning Curve*. Match the phrases in the box with the people.

has tried parachuting   works as a chef   went to college with Jack   left a job to travel and work

3 ▶ 6.12 Read the statements below. Who says each one: Simon or Kate? Watch or listen again and check.

1. We should see the world when we're young. ____
2. You should never leave a job without having another one. ____
3. There aren't that many jobs for vets at the zoo. ____
4. I can go for days without my cell phone. ____

Conversation builder agreeing and disagreeing

Agreeing:
Exactly!   You're right.
I suppose so.   True.
Absolutely!

Disagreeing:
I don't think so.   Oh, come on!
I don't know.   I'm not sure about that.

4 A Read the Conversation builder. Which expressions did Simon and Kate use to agree/disagree?

B ▶ 6.13 Put the phrases in the correct columns from the Conversation builder. Listen, check, and repeat.

agree/disagree strongly	agree/disagree	agree/disagree with doubts

54

agreeing and disagreeing ■ taking turns **SPEAKING** SKILLS **6D**

5 **A** Look at sentences 1–6. Check (✓) the box to show how much you agree or disagree.

	agree strongly	agree	not sure	disagree	disagree strongly
1 English is a difficult language to learn.	☐	☐	☐	☐	☐
2 We should all give up watching TV.	☐	☐	☐	☐	☐
3 People use cell phones too much.	☐	☐	☐	☐	☐
4 True love only exists in fairy tales.	☐	☐	☐	☐	☐
5 Music was better 20 years ago.	☐	☐	☐	☐	☐
6 Money doesn't make you happy.	☐	☐	☐	☐	☐

B In pairs, read the sentences to each other and agree or disagree using the phrases from the Conversation builder. Explain your reasons.

6 ▶ 6.14 Watch or listen to the second part of the show. What is Jack's news?

7 ▶ 6.14 Choose the correct options to answer the questions. Watch or listen again to check.
1 What does Jack think about Alyssa's plan to travel to Africa?
  a It's a good idea.   b It could be dangerous.   c It will be difficult without Wi-Fi.
2 What does Jack say about being on social media?
  a It's not expensive.   b It's risky.   c It will be good for his business.
3 What does Simon say about cooking?
  a He's bad at it.   b He's good at it.   c He can only cook eggs.
4 What do Kate and Simon offer to do?
  a help Jack cook   b pay for the dessert   c help Jack to make a video

> 🔧 **Skill** taking turns
>
> **When people talk in groups, they take turns.**
> • Wait until someone has finished their point before you start speaking.
> • If you start speaking at the same time, stop and apologize.
> • If someone isn't speaking much, encourage them to join in.

8 **A** ▶ 6.15 Read the Skill box. Listen and repeat the phrases when you hear the beep.
1 Sorry, go on.   3 Sorry, you were saying?
2 Don't you think, Jack?   4 What about you, Simon?

B Why do the speakers use phrases 1–4?

9 ▶ 6.16 Listen and check (✓) the conversation in which the speaker waits the right amount of time before speaking.

Conversation 1 ☐   Conversation 2 ☐   Conversation 3 ☐

Go to Communication practice: All students, page 174

10 **A** PREPARE Choose one of the statements and decide if you agree or disagree. Think of arguments and examples to support your opinion.
1 If you want a good job, you need to speak English.   3 There is a perfect partner for everyone.
2 Friends are more important than families.   4 Sugar is dangerous for our health.

B PRACTICE In groups of three, take turns talking about the statements you chose. Encourage other students to give their opinions and be polite.

C PERSONAL BEST Whose arguments did you agree with the most? Why?

Personal Best Write a conversation where two people disagree about something strongly.

55

5 and 6 REVIEW and PRACTICE

Grammar

1 Choose the correct options to complete the sentences.

1. I'd get together with her if I _____ more time.
   a. had
   b. 'll have
   c. have

2. Be careful! You _____ risks.
   a. won't take
   b. shouldn't take
   c. wouldn't take

3. If it's cold tomorrow, I _____ a jacket.
   a. 'd take
   b. 'll take
   c. take

4. If the bus _____, I'll walk to work.
   a. doesn't arrive
   b. didn't arrive
   c. won't arrive

5. A: I have an interview today. How do I look?
   B: I _____ wear those shoes.
   a. don't think you should
   b. think you should to
   c. shouldn't think you

6. Have you _____ to Mexico?
   a. ever been
   b. ever go
   c. went ever

7. What _____ if you saw an accident?
   a. did you do
   b. will you do
   c. would you do

8. I _____ Turkish food.
   a. never have eaten
   b. have never eaten
   c. have eaten never

2 Use the words in parentheses to write sentences that mean the same as the first sentence.

1. I haven't eaten sushi in my life.
   I _____ sushi. (never)

2. I don't have my phone, so I can't call him.
   If _____ my phone, I _____ him. (had / call)

3. It's a bad idea to go to the party.
   I _____ you _____ to the party. (think / should)

4. I think you should look for a new job.
   If _____ you, I _____ for a new job. (were / look)

5. They might lose the game. Mario will be upset if that happens.
   If _____ the game, Mario _____ happy. (lose / be)

6. Where's Julio? Is he in Paris for the meeting?
   Where's Julio? _____ to Paris for the meeting? (has / go)

3 Complete the text with the correct forms of the verbs in parentheses.

The truth about Murphy's Law

Have you ever ¹_____ (drop) a piece of toast and wondered why it always seems to land with the buttered side on the floor? Or, when you leave the house in the morning, have you ever ²_____ (think), "If I ³_____ (take) an umbrella, it ⁴_____ (not rain), but if I ⁵_____ (not take) one, it ⁶_____ (rain)?" These are examples of Murphy's Law, the law that says, "If something can go wrong, it will." We've all ⁷_____ (have) experiences like this, but what ⁸_____ we _____ (should / do) about it?

Well, maybe we ⁹_____ (not should / worry) too much. Professor Richard Dawkins, at the University of Oxford, doesn't think Murphy's Law is really true. He says that certain things happen all the time, but we only notice them when they cause us problems. Imagine if you ¹⁰_____ (be) outside filming a video and a noisy plane ¹¹_____ (fly) by, you ¹²_____ (think) it was Murphy's Law. However, planes fly by all the time. It's only when they cause us a problem that we notice them!

So next time something goes wrong, don't blame Murphy; think positively and try to remember the other times that things went well.

Vocabulary

1 Match the words in the box with the definitions.

> ache   give up   take a break   make an excuse
> lonely   miserable   run out of   roots   valley
> have a talk

1. low land between mountains _____
2. to finish, use, or sell all of something _____
3. to talk together in a friendly way _____
4. to rest for a moment before starting again _____
5. very unhappy _____
6. to stop _____
7. a pain somewhere in your body _____
8. sad because you are alone _____
9. the parts of a tree that are underground _____
10. to explain why something bad happened _____

REVIEW and PRACTICE **5** and **6**

2 Choose the correct words to complete the sentences.
1 When will you find _____ your results?
  a out   b about   c of
2 I _____ my best, and that's all I can do.
  a did   b made   c was
3 He's very _____ today. He's not worried at all.
  a calm   b guilty   c upset
4 I'll _____ bus schedules on the Internet.
  a fill out   b take care of   c look up
5 She broke my laptop. She feels really _____ .
  a guilty   b envious   c jealous
6 I _____ a big argument with my parents.
  a had   b did   c made

3 Circle the word that is different. Explain your answer.
1 backache   earache   sore throat   nosebleed
2 cliff   sunset   lightning   thunderstorm
3 flu   cold   cough   stressed
4 calm   upset   confident   cheerful
5 a mistake   a talk   a good time   an argument
6 lake   cave   river   stream
7 lonely   guilty   miserable   delighted
8 a break   an effort a chance   your time

4 Complete the conversation with the words in the box.

| waves | wildlife | hurt | made | cut | take |
| down | have | rainforest | rocks | | |

Matt Hi, Kerry. Did you ¹_____ a good time on vacation?
Kerry Not really. In fact, it was a disaster.
Matt Oh no! What happened?
Kerry Well, I tried surfing for the first time, but the ²_____ were too big!
Matt Did you have an accident?
Kerry Yes, I hit some ³_____ that were under the water and I ⁴_____ my leg.
Matt Oh dear! Does it still ⁵_____ now?
Kerry Yes, it does. And another day, I went on a boat trip in the ⁶_____ to see the animals that live there, but the boat broke ⁷_____ , and we had to wait for hours for another one to rescue us.
Matt Did you see any ⁸_____ ?
Kerry Just mosquitoes!
Matt Oh no. That's too bad!
Kerry I think I ⁹_____ a mistake. Next year, I'm going to stay home and not ¹⁰_____ any chances.

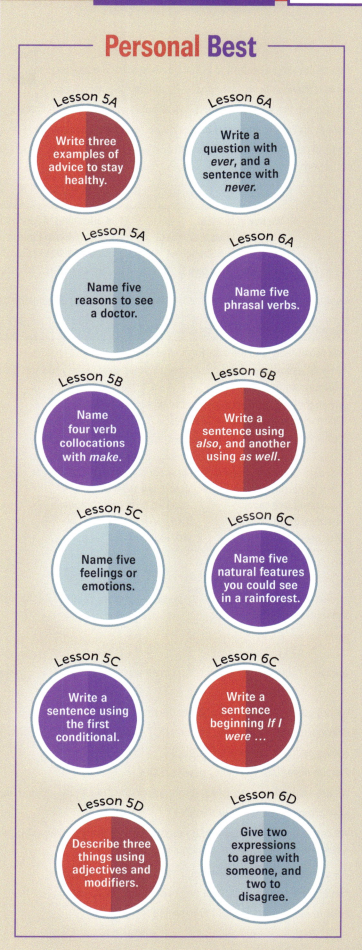

57

GRAMMAR PRACTICE

1A Simple present

We use the simple present to talk about things that are always true.

My best friend is from Argentina.   He doesn't like tomatoes.

We also use the simple present to talk about regular routines and habits.

I talk to my best friend every day.   We go for coffee once a week.

We form negatives and questions with *don't/doesn't* and *do/does* + the base form of the verb.

▶ 1.4	I / you / we / they	he / she / it
+	We **live** in Istanbul.	Carlos **lives** in Santiago.
−	They **don't live** in Quebec.	Megan **doesn't live** in Sydney.
?	**Do** you **live** in Shanghai?	**Does** she **live** in Cairo?
Y/N	Yes, I **do**. / No, I **don't**.	Yes, she **does**. / No, she **doesn't**.

We usually add *s* to the base form to make the third person singular (*he/she/it*) form.

Spelling rules for third person singular (*he / she / it*)
We usually add *-s* to the base form. *live ⇨ lives*
When the base form ends in consonant + *y*, we change the *y* to *i* and then add *-es*. *study ⇨ studies*
When the base form ends in *-sh*, *-ch*, *-x*, *-s* we add *-es*. *finish ⇨ finishes   watch ⇨ watches*
Some verbs are irregular. *go ⇨ goes   do ⇨ does   have ⇨ has*

> **Look!** The verbs *be* and *can* are irregular in the simple present.
> *I'm a generous person.*   *David can swim well.*
> *You aren't late today.*   *You can't use this computer.*
> *Are they good friends?*   *Can you help us?*
> *Yes, they are.*   *No, we can't.*

Adverbs and expressions of frequency

We use adverbs of frequency with the simple present to talk about habits and routines.

100% ——————————————————— **0%**

always   usually   often   sometimes   hardly ever   never

We put adverbs of frequency before the main verb.

I always see my friends after classes. NOT ~~Always I see my friends after classes~~.

But we put them after the verb *be*.

They're never late. NOT ~~They never are late~~.

We use *How often …?* to ask questions about how frequently actions happen.

How often do you see your friends?

We can also use expressions of frequency, such as *every day/week/month* or *once a week/month/year* to talk about regular routines.

We usually use expressions of frequency at the end of sentences.

I meet Julia once a week. NOT ~~I meet once a week Julia~~.

I talk to her every day. NOT ~~I talk every day to her~~.

---

1 Complete the sentences with the correct form of the verbs in parentheses.

1 I _____ coffee. (not like)
2 _____ they _____ computer games with you? (play)
3 Luca _____ work at 6:00 p.m. (finish)
4 We _____ fun together. (have)
5 You _____ my best friend. (not know)
6 _____ Robert _____ with you? (work)
7 Constanza is really shy. She _____ in class. (not speak)
8 My mom _____ a lot about her children. (worry)
9 _____ you_____ me with this? (can / help)
10 Raul _____ very patient. (not be)

2 Rewrite the sentences and questions with the adverbs of frequency in the correct place.

1 We go for coffee after class. (sometimes)
_____
2 Do you talk to your best friend every day? (usually)
_____
3 My best friend is there for me, day or night. (always)
_____
4 How do you talk to your best friend? (often)
_____
5 My roommates are in our apartment. (hardly ever)
_____
6 Lucia works hard. (never)
_____

3 Put the words in the correct order to make sentences and questions.

1 your / often / friends / do / see / how / you ?
_____
2 usually / drink / doesn't / Luis / coffee
_____
3 evening / Sandra / every / studies
_____
4 me / friends / to / always / my / listen
_____
5 day / we / home / every / at / cook
_____
6 you / dentist / often / the / how / see / do ?
_____
7 week / bedroom / a / clean / times / I / my / three
_____
8 often / on / you / how / vacation / go / do ?
_____

112

◀ Go back to page 5

GRAMMAR PRACTICE

1C Present continuous

We use the present continuous to talk about things that are happening now.

My brother is taking a shower right now.
Are you reading a good book at the moment?

We also use the present continuous to talk about things that are temporary.

I'm staying at my parents' house this semester.
She isn't working in the office this month.

We form the present continuous with the verb *be* + the *-ing* form of the main verb.

▶ 1.12	I	he / she / it	you / we / they
+	I'm **reading** a book.	Daniel's **sleeping**.	We're all **wearing** glasses!
−	I'm **not working** in the office today.	My cousin **isn't staying** with me this week.	We **aren't using** this room now.
?	**Am** I **dreaming**?	**Is** she **studying** French this month?	**Are** you **watching** TV?
Y/N	Yes, I **am**. / No, I'm **not**.	Yes, she **is**. / No, she **isn't**.	Yes, we **are**. / No, we **aren't**.

We usually add *-ing* to the base form to make the *-ing* form.

Spelling rules for the *-ing* form

We usually add *-ing* to the base form. *play* ⇨ *playing* *talk* ⇨ *talking*

When a verb ends in *e*, we omit the *e* before adding *-ing*.
take ⇨ *taking* *live* ⇨ *living*

When a verb ends in consonant + vowel + consonant, we double the final consonant before adding *-ing*. *sit* ⇨ *sitting* *plan* ⇨ *planning*

Look! We often use the present continuous with time expressions, such as *(right) now, today, this week/month/year, at the moment.*
I'm studying economics now.
Today, they're not working very much.

Simple present and present continuous

We use the simple present to talk about things that are always true, and the present continuous to talk about things that are temporary.

Rebecca lives in Mexico City, but this month she's living in New York.

We use the simple present to talk about things that happen regularly and the present continuous to talk about things that are happening now.

I usually take the bus to work, but today I'm taking a taxi.

However, there are some verbs that describe a state rather than an action. We don't normally use these verbs in the present continuous.

Maria hates the new TV series. NOT ~~Maria is hating the new TV series~~.
My teacher doesn't think it's correct. NOT ~~My teacher isn't thinking it's correct~~.
I have a rental car at the moment. NOT ~~I'm having a rental car at the moment~~.

State verbs

Feelings	like, love, hate, want, prefer, need
Thoughts and opinions	know, believe, remember, forget, understand, think
States	be, exist, seem, look like, belong, own, have

1 Write sentences using the present continuous.

1 My sister / travel / in Asia / right now

_____

2 Ivan / not work / this week

_____

3 What / you / learn about / in your history class?

_____

4 They / plan / a trip to Mexico

_____

5 I / not shout

_____

6 you / use / that chair?

_____

7 she / wear / a scarf?

_____

8 I / not go running / this month

_____

2 Complete the sentences with the present continuous or the simple present form of the verbs in parentheses.

1 We can't have a picnic today. It _____ . (rain)
2 She often _____ her friends here. (meet)
3 Turn that music down! The children _____ . (sleep)
4 The trains are really busy because everyone _____ to work right now. (go)
5 It's amazing how much she _____ her mom. (look like)
6 Can you turn off the TV, please, if you _____ it? (not watch)
7 He _____ a suit to work, except when he has an important meeting. (not wear)
8 I can't talk while I _____ . I'll call you later. (drive)

3 Complete the text with the present continuous or the simple present form of the verbs in parentheses.

Ella Richards is the granddaughter of Keith Richards, who ¹_____ (play) guitar with the Rolling Stones. Ella is 18 and a model, and she ²_____ (appear) in a series of ads for a fashion company at the moment. She ³_____ (live) at home, with her mom, dad, and younger brother, but this week she ⁴_____ (work) in London, and she ⁵_____ (stay) at her grandmother's house. In our photo, she ⁶_____ (wear) a black dress with flowers, and she ⁷_____ (carry) a handbag. She says that when she's older, she ⁸_____ (want) to be a spy!

◀ Go back to page 8

113

GRAMMAR PRACTICE

2A Simple past

We use the simple past to talk about completed actions in the past.

I bought a new camera yesterday.
Emma didn't come to work last week.
Did you see Lucia at the party?

We form negatives and questions with *didn't* and *did* + the base form of the verb.

▶ 2.1	Regular verbs	Irregular verbs
+	We **walked** to school yesterday.	We **took** a lot of photos.
−	I **didn't study** science in college.	He **didn't go** shopping last week.
?	**Did** he **use** his own camera?	**Did** you **meet** anyone interesting?
Y/N	Yes, he **did**.	No, I **didn't**.

We usually add *-ed* to regular verbs to make the positive form of the simple past.

Spelling rules for regular simple past positive forms
We usually add **-ed** to the verb. *play ⇨ played   watch ⇨ watched*
When a verb ends in **e**, we add **-d**. *dance ⇨ danced   live ⇨ lived*
When a verb ends in consonant + **y**, we change the **y** to **i** and then we add **-ed**. *study ⇨ studied*
When a verb ends in consonant + vowel + consonant, we double the final consonant and then add **-ed**. *stop ⇨ stopped   plan ⇨ planned*

Many common verbs have irregular simple past positive forms.

go ⇨ went   have ⇨ had   take ⇨ took

Look! The verbs *be* and *can* are irregular in the simple past.	
I was at the party.	*We could see the house.*
She wasn't here.	*He couldn't come to class.*
Were you happy?	*Could you speak French when you were younger?*
Yes, I was.	*No, I couldn't.*

Time expressions

We often use time expressions with the simple past to say when an action happened. Time expressions can go at the end or at the beginning of sentences.

Last year, the president traveled to Europe.
The president traveled to Europe last year.
NOT ~~The president traveled last year to Europe~~.

▶ 2.2	Time expressions
at + times	The train arrived **at 6 o'clock**.
in + seasons, months, years	They traveled **in the summer**. **In 2015**, we moved to Portugal.
last + *night/week/month/year*	**Last night**, I saw a good game on TV. We went there **last year**.
on + days, dates, *the weekend*	What did you do **on Monday**? Did you do anything special **on July 4th?** I went to the movies **on the weekend.**
seconds, minutes, hours, days, weeks, months, years + **ago**	**An hour ago**, Kevin was here. I saw him **three days ago.**
yesterday	I saw her **yesterday.**

---

1 Complete the sentences with the correct simple past form of the verbs.

1 They _____ to speak Spanish in Colombia. (learn)
2 _____ you _____ Hannah yesterday? (see)
3 We _____ this photo from the top of that building. (take)
4 I _____ to class last week. (not go)
5 _____ you _____ the movie? (enjoy)
6 How annoying! Elise _____ her e-mails last night. (not check)
7 _____ Paula _____ you on Monday? (call)
8 I _____ in a restaurant five years ago. (work)

2 A Write simple past questions.

1 what / you / do / yesterday?
   _____
2 your sister / go / on vacation / with you / last year?
   _____
3 when / you / finish / the project?
   _____
4 you / have / a smartphone / ten years ago?
   _____
5 when / Mario / take / the photo?
   _____
6 where / be / you / on Monday / at 10:00 a.m.?
   _____

B Match answers a–f with questions 1–6.

a I finished it a few days ago. _____
b Yes, I did. It was very expensive. _____
c I went to a friend's house and watched a movie. _____
d I was in my car, driving to work. _____
e No, she didn't. She stayed at home. _____
f He took it last month when he was in Poland. _____

3 Choose the correct options to complete the sentences.

1 We didn't take any photos *on / in / at* the summer.
2 I bought this phone a few years *ago / last / past*.
3 We moved to a new apartment *on / in / at* August.
4 Did you see Andrés in town *yesterday / last day / day ago*?
5 The concert started *in / on / at* 9:00 p.m.
6 Monica and Julieta went to the movies *in / at / on* Saturday.
7 Did your college course finish *in / on / at* July 5th?
8 They met in a café *ago / last / past* night.

114

◀ Go back to page 13

2C Question forms

When we ask for specific information, we use a question word, such as *who*, *where*, *when*, *how*, or *why*.

Where does Maria live?	She lives in Germany.
How did they get here?	They came by car.
Why are you wearing a coat?	I'm wearing it because I'm cold.

When we ask for a *Yes* or *No* answer, we don't use a question word.

Do you like coffee?	Yes, I do.
Did the train arrive late?	No, it didn't.
Is Ling Mai from China?	Yes, she is.

With most verbs, we use an auxiliary verb.

▶ 2.9

question word	auxiliary verb	subject	main verb
Where	does	your brother	go to college?
	Do	you	remember your elementary school?
How	did	your sister	get her first job?
	Did	Gustavo	see you yesterday?
Which book	are	you	reading right now?
	Is	Karla	looking forward to the trip?

With the verb *be*, we don't use an auxiliary verb and the subject comes after *be*.

▶ 2.10

question word	be	subject	
Where	are	you	from?
	Is	the meeting	in March?
Why	was	the computer	broken?
	Were	you	at the party?

Look! We usually put prepositions at the end of questions, after the main verb.
Who did she get married to? NOT ~~To who did she get married?~~
What are you worried about? NOT ~~About what are you worried?~~

We use *how* in different ways when we ask questions.

How—to ask about the way of doing something
How do you travel to work?

How often—to ask about frequency
How often do you wash your hair?

How long—to ask about duration
How long is the movie?

How old—to ask about age
How old were you when you moved here?

How much/many—to ask about quantity
How much money do you have?

How + adjective—to ask about a specific quality
How deep is the swimming pool?

GRAMMAR PRACTICE

1 Put the words in the correct order to make questions.
1 often / gym / how / you / the / go / do / to
   _____?
2 go / to / which / did / college / they
   _____?
3 weekend / go / where / on / you / the / did
   _____?
4 thinking / what / you / about / are
   _____?
5 whose / today / it / is / birthday
   _____?
6 to / work / how / get / she / does
   _____?
7 who / you / at / are / looking
   _____?
8 for / class / why / late / you / were
   _____?

2 Write questions for the answers.
1 He was born in Belo Horizonte in Brazil.
   Where _____?
2 They grew up with their grandparents.
   Who _____?
3 She met her husband at a party.
   Where _____?
4 They have five children.
   How many _____?
5 He retired because of poor health.
   Why _____?
6 At the moment, he's working on a new project.
   What _____?

3 A Put the words from the box in the correct place to complete the interviewer's questions.

you	did	it	to	with	are

1 Where you from?
2 When you start singing?
3 What type of music do you listen?
4 Is difficult to write songs?
5 In the future, which musicians do you hope to work?
6 Do enjoy being famous?

B Match answers a–f with questions 1–6.
a I love all music—rock and pop, especially. ____
b I don't know. I just sing the songs. ____
c I was born in Puerto Rico, but I grew up in New York. ____
d I'm planning on working with Shakira soon. ____
e Yes, I do. I love it! ____
f I started singing classes when I was six years old. ____

◀ Go back to page 17

115

GRAMMAR PRACTICE

3A Comparatives, superlatives, (not) as ... as

Comparatives

We use comparative adjectives + *than* to compare things.

Helen is taller than Jason.
The train is more expensive than the bus.

We can also use *less* + adjective + *than* to compare things.

The train is less crowded than the bus. = *The bus is more crowded than the train.*
The subway is less expensive than the train. = *The subway is cheaper than the train.*

(not) as ... as

We use *as ... as* with adjectives to say two things are the same.

Sofia is as tall as Jasmine.   *The train is as fast as the bus.*

We use *not as ... as* with adjectives to say two things are different.

Sofia isn't as tall as Helen. = *Sofia is less tall than Helen.*
The bus isn't as expensive as the train. = *The bus is less expensive than the train.*

> **Look!** After comparatives or *(not) as ... as*, we can use an object pronoun or a subject pronoun + auxiliary verb.
> *Marcos is faster than me. / Marcos is faster than I am.*
> *Claudia is more relaxed than her. / Claudia is more relaxed than she is.*

Superlatives

We use superlative adjectives to say that something is more than all the others in a group.

Helen is the tallest in her class.
The train is the most expensive way to travel around this city.

We can also use *the least* + adjective to say something is less than all the others in a group.

It's the least dangerous way to travel. = *It's the safest way to travel.*

Spelling rules for comparative and superlative adjectives
When an adjective is one syllable, we add *-er / -est*.   fast ⇒ faster ⇒ fastest
When a one-syllable adjective ends in consonant + vowel + consonant, we double the final consonant and add *-er / -est*.   hot ⇒ hotter ⇒ hottest
When an adjective ends in consonant + ***y***, we change the ***y*** to ***i*** and then add *-er / -est*.   easy ⇒ easier ⇒ easiest
When an adjective is two or more syllables, we use ***more/most*** + adjective.   comfortable ⇒ more comfortable ⇒ most comfortable
Some comparatives are irregular.   good ⇒ better ⇒ best   bad ⇒ worse ⇒ worst   far ⇒ further/farther ⇒ furthest/farthest

▶ 3.2

Comparatives	Fish is **healthier than** meat. I'm much **more/less patient than** you.
(not) as ... as	Melissa is **as friendly as** her sister. It is**n't as warm as** it was yesterday.
Superlatives	This is **the fastest** car in the world. I bought **the most/least expensive** phone in the store.

---

1. Complete the sentences with the comparative or superlative form of the adjectives in parentheses.
   1. The Torre Latino is the _____ place for a view of Mexico City. (good)
   2. I can't believe you're _____ than me! (old)
   3. My apartment is _____ from the park than yours. (far)
   4. I think Tokyo is the _____ city I know. (interesting)
   5. Is Beijing _____ than Tokyo? (big)
   6. Dubai is one of the _____ airports in the world. (busy)

2. Complete the second sentence with *(not) as ... as* so it means the same as the first sentence.
   1. Your new apartment is bigger than your old apartment.
      Your old apartment is _____ your new apartment.
   2. Moscow is more famous than São Paulo.
      São Paulo is _____ Moscow.
   3. The subway and the bus are equally crowded.
      The subway is _____ the bus.
   4. I think this part of town is livelier than downtown.
      Downtown is _____ this part of town.

3. Look at the information. Write three sentences using the adjectives in the boxes.

Hotel Romeo	Hotel Brooklyn	Hotel Cruz
$500	$300	$125

   `cheap   expensive`

   1. Hotel Cruz is _____ hotel.
   2. Hotel Romeo is _____ hotel.
   3. Hotel Brooklyn is _____ Hotel Romeo, but it isn't as _____ Hotel Cruz.

   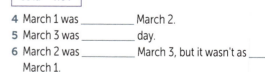

   March 1, 10°   March 2, 15°   March 3, 25°

   `cold   hot`

   4. March 1 was _____ March 2.
   5. March 3 was _____ day.
   6. March 2 was _____ March 3, but it wasn't as _____ March 1.

   Mumbai   Madrid   Buenos Aires

   `busy   quiet`

   7. Mumbai is _____ city.
   8. Buenos Aires is _____ city.
   9. Madrid isn't as _____ Mumbai, but it's _____ Buenos Aires.

◀ Go back to page 23

3C Past continuous

We use the past continuous to describe actions in progress at a particular time in the past.

I was sleeping at 7:00 this morning.
I was working at my desk when the telephone rang.

We form the past continuous with the simple past of the verb *be* + the *-ing* form of the main verb.

▶ 3.10	I / he / she / it	you / we / they
+	I **was watching** TV at 6:00 last night.	We **were walking** home when it started to rain.
–	It **wasn't raining** when I got to work.	The players **weren't playing** very well.
?	**Was** she **working** at this office when you met her?	**Were** you **living** here at the beginning of the year?
Y/N	Yes, she **was**. / No, she **wasn't**.	Yes, we **were**. / No, we **weren't**.

Past continuous and simple past

We use the simple past to describe completed actions in the past, for example a series of actions.

Yesterday, I woke up, I had breakfast, and then I took a shower.

I woke up.   I had breakfast.   I took a shower.

We use the past continuous with the simple past to describe an action that was in progress when a completed action happened.

The action in progress can continue.
I was having breakfast when I heard the new song on the radio. = I continued having breakfast.

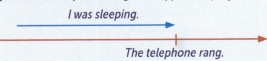
I was having breakfast.
I heard the new song on the radio.

Or the action in progress may stop.
I was sleeping when the telephone rang. = I stopped sleeping.

I was sleeping.
The telephone rang.

We can also use two past continuous verbs together to show that two actions were happening at the same time.
I was cooking while Steve was doing his homework.

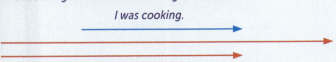
I was cooking.
Steve was doing his homework.

Look! We often use **when** and **while** in sentences with the past continuous.
I broke my leg while I was playing soccer.
I was playing soccer when I broke my leg.
While I was playing soccer, I broke my leg.

GRAMMAR PRACTICE

1 Complete the conversations with the past continuous form of the verbs in parentheses.

1 A _____ (you / watch) TV just now?
   B No, I wasn't. It was the radio.
2 A Why didn't you see Paula and Mark?
   B They _____ (walk) the dog.
3 A Why was the boss angry with Nigel?
   B He _____ (not work) fast enough.
4 A Why didn't you play tennis yesterday?
   B It _____ (rain) all day.
5 A Did you ask Thomas to come to the party?
   B Yes, I talked to him while we _____ (have) lunch.

2 Change one verb in each sentence to the past continuous.

1 We had dinner outside while we stayed in Rome.
   _____
2 When Lisa crossed the street, she dropped her phone and it broke.
   _____
3 We had dinner outside when it started to rain.
   _____
4 I didn't listen when the teacher told us about the exam next week.
   _____
5 While we sat in the taxi, we checked the address of the hotel.
   _____

3 Choose the correct form of the verbs to complete the text about a movie of Alastair Humphreys' new adventure.

Into The Empty Quarter

In September 2012, Alastair Humphreys [1]*trained / was training* for an expedition to the South Pole. Unfortunately, he [2]*found out / was finding out* that the trip couldn't take place because there wasn't enough money. So he [3]*had to / was having to* find a new adventure quickly. One day, he [4]*looked / was looking* through his adventure books when he [5]*found / was finding* the answer —a book named *Arabian Sands* about Wilfred Thesiger's trip across the Arabian desert in the 1940s. Alastair immediately [6]*contacted / was contacting* another explorer, Leon McCarron, and they started planning how to walk more than 1,600 kilometers across the desert. They [7]*began / were beginning* the trip in November 2012, and were home before the end of the year. But this time they [8]*filmed / were filming* all their adventures, too. *Into The Empty Quarter* is their story.

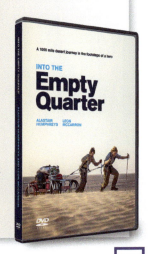

◀ Go back to page 27

117

GRAMMAR PRACTICE

4A *will*, *may*, and *might* for predictions

We use *will* and *won't* (=*will not*) + the base form to make predictions about the future. We usually use the contraction *'ll* after personal pronouns, such as *I, he, she,* etc. and after *there*.

It'll be sunny tomorrow.   It definitely won't rain.
There'll be lots of traffic tonight.   She won't be here on time.

We often use *probably* to say that the prediction is less sure. *Probably* comes after *will* and before *won't*.

I'll probably go to the gym tonight.
You probably won't see Karen tomorrow.

We use *may* and *might* + the base form to say that a prediction is possible. There is no difference in meaning between *may* and *might*.

He may be hungry when he gets home.
They might not serve any food on the flight.

We don't use *may* or *might* to make questions.

Will the exam be difficult? NOT ~~Might the exam be difficult?~~

We can use *may* and *might* to reply to questions.

Will he get the job? He might. I'm not sure.
Will it rain tomorrow? It might, or it might not!

▶ 4.3	will	may	might
+	It**'ll rain** tomorrow.	It **may snow** tomorrow.	It **might be** windy.
–	She **won't pass** the exam.	Kelly **may not come**.	Jorge **might not arrive** on time.
?	**Will** she **be** the next president?		
Y/N	Yes, she **will**. / No, she **won't**.	Yes, she **may**. / No, she **may not**.	Yes, she **might**. / No, she **might not**.

Look! We often make predictions with *I think* … or *I don't think* … to show it is our opinion.
I think he'll win the race.
I don't think she'll lose her job. NOT ~~I think she won't lose her job~~.

---

1 Write sentences using the correct form of *will*, *may*, and *might*.

1 It / probably / rain / tomorrow (will)
   _____

2 You / need / your car (may not)
   _____

3 I / don't think / we / see / you later (will)
   _____

4 We / have time / to go for coffee? (will)
   _____

5 She / come / to the meeting later (might)
   _____

6 They / probably / go / on vacation next year (won't)
   _____

7 I / think / there / be / lots of people / at the party (will)
   _____

8 What do you think / happen? (will)
   _____

2 Choose the correct words to complete the sentences.

1 They *will / might* go on vacation to Colombia, but they don't have much money, so they *'ll / might* probably just stay at home.

2 I don't think England *will / may* win the next World Cup. I'm sure it *will / may* be Germany.

3 I probably *won't / may not* go to the movies, but I *'ll / may* be able to meet you afterward. Can I text you later to let you know?

4 I'm sure *you 'll / might* pass your exam. *Will / Might* they tell you your grade right away?

5 It's certain that robots *will / may* become a part of all our lives. Who knows—a robot *will / may* even become president!

6 I know that *you 'll / might* really like Michael. You *'ll / might* meet him this weekend, although I'm not sure because his father's not well at the moment.

3 Complete the predictions with *will* or *won't* and the verbs in the box.

> buy   choose   come   become   exist   use
> go shopping   increase   live   understand

What will the world be like in 2050?

1 The world's population _____ to more than nine billion people.

2 Scientists _____ more about diseases and people _____ longer.

3 Parents _____ the sex of their baby.

4 We _____ oil and gas for electricity. Most of our energy _____ from solar power.

5 Some islands _____ anymore as sea levels rise. Some animals _____ extinct.

6 People _____ downtown. Instead, they _____ everything online.

118

◀ Go back to page 31

GRAMMAR PRACTICE

4C *be going to* and present continuous

We use *be going to* + the base form to talk about future plans.

What are you going to do tonight?
I'm going to watch a movie on TV.

▶ 4.7	I	he / she / it	you / we / they
+	I**'m going to look** for a new job.	The company**'s going to move** to a new office.	We**'re going to design** a new product.
–	I**'m not going to take** the bus tomorrow morning.	Hans **isn't going to buy** a new car.	My friends **aren't going to visit** me next year.
?	**Am** I **going to work** harder next year?	**Is** she **going to study** politics next year?	**Are** they **going to cook** dinner tonight?
Y/N	Yes, I **am**. / No, I **'m not**.	Yes, she **is**. / No, she **isn't**.	Yes, they **are**. / No, they **aren't**.

> **Look!** When the main verb is *go*, we usually omit *to go*.
> *Are you going (to go) swimming tonight?*
> *Maria is going (to go) abroad next year.*

When we talk about arrangements with a fixed place and time, we often use the present continuous.

What are you doing tonight?
I'm meeting Charlie and Susie downtown.

But it is also correct to use *be going to*.

What are you going to do tonight?
I'm going to meet Charlie and Susie downtown.

Future time expressions

We often use future time expressions with *be going to* and the present continuous. The time expressions usually come at the beginning or at the end of a sentence.

Sandra is going to help us next week.
Next week, Sandra is going to help us.

▶ 4.8	
next + *week/month/year*, etc.	We're going to buy a new house **next year**.
In ... two days'/five years' time	**In three weeks' time**, we're meeting with our colleagues from Colombia.
tonight	What are you doing **tonight**?
tomorrow	I'm not going to do anything exciting **tomorrow**.
the day after tomorrow	Peter is going to give a presentation at the conference **the day after tomorrow**.

1 Write sentences using *be going to*.

1 he / buy / some tickets for the soccer game
_____

2 the actor / make / a new TV series / next year
_____

3 they / go / to Spain / on vacation this year?
_____

4 she / not use / an architect
_____

5 where / you / sit?
_____

6 he / ask / his manager about the problem
_____

7 I / go / to the gym tonight
_____

8 you / drive or take the bus?
_____

2 Look at Kelly's day planner. Make sentences using the present continuous.

9:00 a.m.	new manager (Josie) starts
10:00 a.m.	introduce Josie to the team
11:00 a.m.	~~visit the factory~~
1:00 p.m.	have lunch with Andy
2:00 p.m.	pick up new sofa!
6:30 p.m.	~~go to yoga class~~ canceled

1 Kelly's new manager, Josie, _____ at 9:00.
2 At 10:00, Kelly _____ .
3 Is she _____ at 11:00? No, she isn't.
4 At 1:00, Kelly and Andy _____ together.
5 At 2:00, she _____ a new sofa.
6 She _____ her yoga class tonight. It was canceled.

3 Choose the correct options to complete the sentences.

1 Hi, Bob. What ____ on June 18th next year?
   a you are going to do   **b** are you doing
   c do you do
2 It's Mom's 70th birthday and we ____ a big party. You're invited!
   a 're having   **b** have   **c** 're going
3 The whole family ____ there, and lots of Mom's friends.
   a is being   **b** is doing   **c** is going to be
4 I'm sure everyone ____ a good time.
   a has   **b** is having   **c** is going to have
5 We want it to be a secret, so we ____ Mom.
   a are telling   **b** don't tell   **c** aren't going to tell
6 I ____ a big birthday cake for the party. Do you know a good pastry shop?
   a 'm going to order   **b** order   **c** 'm order

◄ Go back to page 34

119

GRAMMAR PRACTICE

5A *should/shouldn't*

We use *should* and *shouldn't* + the base form to ask for and give advice and recommendations.

Where should I go on vacation?
You should stay in this country.
You shouldn't go abroad. It's too expensive.

▶ 5.2	I / you / he / she / it / we / they
+	You **should see** a doctor.
−	Rachel **shouldn't drink** so much coffee.
?	**Should** I **buy** some new shoes?
Y/N	Yes, you **should**. / No, you **shouldn't**.

We often use *I think* and *I don't think* with *should* to show our opinion.

What do you think I should do?
I think you should stay in bed.
I don't think you should go out. NOT *I think you shouldn't go out.*

Other ways of giving advice or recommendations

When we want to give strong advice (or warnings) we use the imperative.
Whatever you do, don't go outside. It's freezing!

For recommendations, we use *why don't you ...?* or *you could* + the base form.
Why don't you put a coat and hat on? It's cold outside.
You could stay inside, where it's nice and warm.

1 Complete the sentences with *should* or *shouldn't* and the verbs in parentheses.

1 He looks really tired. I think he _____ to bed. (go)
2 There's a great new restaurant in town. You _____ it. (try)
3 You _____ so fast. You'll get a stomachache. (not eat)
4 It's Andy's birthday. Do you think we _____ him a present? (buy)
5 She wants to get in shape. She _____ a gym. (join)
6 We _____ so much salt on our food. It's not good for our health. (not put)
7 There's a lot of traffic. I don't think you _____ so fast. (drive)
8 They _____ to him like that. It's rude. (not talk)

2 Complete the sentences with the correct form of *should* and the verbs in the box.

buy   get   get up   lose   spend   study   talk   walk

1 A I'm always late for work.
  B You _____ earlier.
2 A I don't have much money right now.
  B I don't think you _____ those shoes, then.
3 A These pants don't fit me anymore.
  B Do you think you _____ some weight?
4 A I want to improve my English.
  B You _____ the summer in Canada.
5 A My brother wants to be an engineer.
  B He _____ math and physics in college.
6 A I'm stressed at work lately.
  B You _____ to your boss.
7 A You _____ home alone at night.
  B OK, I'll get a taxi.
8 A Do you think I _____ more exercise?
  B Yes, definitely.

3 Put the words in the correct order to make sentences.

1 what / I / don't / do / I / should / know
_____

2 before / the / should / we / leave / house / 9:00
_____

3 take / the / taxi / to / don't / a / airport
_____

4 you / don't / homework / now / why / do / your?
_____

5 job / for / Larry / another / look / could
_____

120

◀ Go back to page 41

5C First conditional

We use the first conditional to talk about the result of a possible future action.
If you help me with my homework, I'll buy you coffee.

There are two parts to a first conditional sentence: an *if* clause to describe the possible future action, and the main clause to describe the result.
If it rains tomorrow, I'll take a taxi to the meeting.

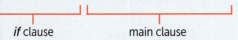

    if clause   main clause

We can put either clause first with no change in meaning. However, if we put the main clause first, we don't use a comma between the two clauses.
If I get sick on vacation, I'll feel miserable.
I'll feel miserable if I get sick on vacation.

We form the *if* clause with *if* + simple present, and we form the main clause with *will* + the base form.

▶ 5.11	*if* clause	main clause
+	**If** I **pass** my driving test,	I'**ll buy** a car.
–	**If** they **don't invite** me to the wedding,	I **won't buy** them a present.
?	**If** you **take** the medicine,	**will** you **feel** better?
Y/N	Yes, I **will**. / No, I **won't**.	

We can also use *may* or *might* + the base form in the main clause to describe results that we are not sure about.
If I get the new job in Shanghai, I might move house.
She may come to the party if she finishes work early.

We use *can* + the base form or *will be able to* + the base form in the main clause to say that a result will be possible.
If I fix my bike, I can ride it to work.
He won't be able to bake a cake if he doesn't buy some eggs.

> **Look!** We can also use the imperative in the main clause to give people instructions for possible situations.
> *Please tell Carla about the new class if you see her tonight.*
> *If you use this computer, don't press this button!*

GRAMMAR PRACTICE

1 Choose the correct words to complete the sentences.
 1 If she *passes / 'll pass* all her exams, her dad *is / will be* really proud.
 2 If we *don't / won't* hurry up, we *miss / 'll miss* the bus.
 3 I *am / 'll be* surprised if his plane *lands / will land* on time tonight.
 4 If he *calls / will call*, *don't / won't* answer the phone.
 5 I *tell / 'll tell* you a secret if you *promise / 'll promise* not to tell anyone.
 6 She *is / 'll be* really disappointed if you *don't / won't* go to her party.
 7 What *do / will* you say if he *asks / 'll ask* you to marry him?
 8 If I *get / 'll get* lonely, *do / will* you give me a call?
 9 He *'s / 'll be* really embarrassed if *he's / he'll be* late to his own wedding.
 10 We *don't / may not* have time for lunch if the meeting *doesn't / won't* finish soon.
 11 *Remind / Will remind* me if I *forget / 'll forget* to call the builder.
 12 If you *don't / won't* leave now, I *call / 'll call* the police.

2 Write first conditional sentences.
 1 I / write to you / if / I / have time
 _____
 2 if / you / see him / you / give him this message, please?
 _____
 3 she / not get her money back / if / she / lose the receipt
 _____
 4 if / he / not get the job / he / be really miserable
 _____
 5 if / you / not fix your car soon / the police / stop you
 _____
 6 my mom / not forgive me / if / I / not remember her birthday
 _____
 7 if / my phone/ ring / not answer it!
 _____
 8 if / she / move to Italy / you / visit her?
 _____
 9 if / you / go for a walk / it / help you to feel better
 _____
 10 if / he / not get too nervous / he / do well on the exam
 _____
 11 they / be late / if / they / not leave soon
 _____
 12 if / I / stand here / you / take a photo of me?
 _____

◀ Go back to page 44

GRAMMAR PRACTICE

6A Present perfect with *ever* and *never*

We use the present perfect to talk about experiences in our lives.

I've read Don Quixote.
He hasn't been to the U.S.
Have they done yoga?

We often use *ever* with questions and *never* instead of the negative to emphasize that we are talking about our lifetime.

Have you ever flown in a helicopter?
I've never eaten a hamburger!

We form the present perfect with the verb *have* and the past participle of the main verb.

▶ 6.3	I / you / we / they	he / she / it
+	I**'ve written** a novel.	Michelle **has been** to China.
-	They **haven't gone swimming** in the river.	Claude **hasn't seen** my new car.
?	**Have** you **tried** this new drink?	**Has** he **worked** as a chef?
Y/N	Yes, I **have**. / No, I **haven't**.	Yes, he **has**. / No, he **hasn't**.

In regular verbs, the past participle is the same as the simple past form.

I cooked pasta yesterday.   *I've never cooked dinner for her.*
He played tennis with her last week.   *Have you ever played the saxophone?*

In some irregular verbs, the past participle is different from the simple past form. For a full list of irregular verbs, see page 175.

I ate toast for breakfast this morning.   *Have you ever eaten Chinese food?*
I saw Roberta at Ruth's party.   *I haven't seen that TV series.*

Present perfect or simple past

We use the present perfect to talk about an experience in our lives and we use the simple past to talk about when a specific event happened.

I've met a movie star.
I met George Clooney in Mexico two years ago.

We often start a conversation with the present perfect. When we ask for more information, or give details, we use the simple past.

Have you ever been to Australia?
Yes, I have. I went there in 2014.
Who did you go with?
I went with my friend, Ella.

---

1 Complete the chart with the correct forms of the verbs.

	Base form	Simple past	Past participle
1	be		been
2	break	broke	
3		cried	cried
4		ate	eaten
5	drive	drove	
6	live		lived
7		sang	sung
8	speak	spoke	
9	stop		stopped
10	walk	walked	

2 Write sentences and questions in the present perfect.

1 you / ever / be / to New Zealand?
_____

2 I / never / eat / hamburgers
_____

3 she / walk / along the Great Wall of China
_____

4 my uncle / not give up / smoking
_____

5 you / ever / watch / the sun rise?
_____

6 we / never / play / rugby
_____

7 he / ever / ask / his boss for a pay raise?
_____

8 my sister / try / to learn English
_____

3 Choose the correct form (present perfect or simple past) to complete the conversation.

Rachel	[1]*Have you ever learned / Did you ever learn* another language?
Sarah	Yes, [2]*I have taught / I taught* myself Spanish about ten years ago.
Rachel	So, [3]*have you ever been / did you ever go* to Spain?
Sarah	No, but [4]*I've been / I went* to South America.
Rachel	Really? When [5]*have you been / did you go* there?
Sarah	Six years ago. [6]*I've been / I went* with John. It was our honeymoon.
Rachel	That's great! [7]*Have you traveled / Did you travel* around a lot when you were there?
Sarah	Yes, [8]*we've visited / we visited* Chile, Argentina, and Brazil. It was amazing!

122   ◀ Go back to page 49

6C Second conditional

We use the second conditional to talk about impossible or very unlikely situations.
If I went climbing in the mountains, I'd take a first-aid kit. (but it's not likely that I'll go climbing in the mountains).

There are two parts to a second conditional sentence: an *if* clause to describe the situation and the main clause to describe the result.

If she had more money, she'd buy a new car.
       if clause   main clause

We can put either clause first with no change in meaning. However, if we put the main clause first, we don't use a comma between the two clauses.
If he spoke German, he would apply for the job.
He would apply for the job if he spoke German.

We form the *if* clause with *if* + simple past, and we form the main clause with *would* + the base form.

Look! We often use *were* instead of *was* in the *if* clause with *I/he/she/it*.
If he were a little taller, the pants would fit him.
I'd take a taxi if I were you.

▶ 6.10	*if* clause	main clause
+	**If** I **knew** the answer,	I**'d tell** you.
−	**If** you **weren't** so impatient,	you **wouldn't have** this problem.
?	**If** it **were** cheaper,	**would** you **buy** it?
Y/N	Yes, I **would**. / No, I **wouldn't**.	

We use *could* + the base form or *would be able to* + the base form in the main clause to say that a result would be possible.
If Alex didn't have so much work, he could go to the party.
Sara would be able to help us if she were here.

Second conditional or first conditional

We can sometimes use either the first conditional or the second conditional, but it depends on if we think a situation is a real possibility, or if we think it's very unlikely/impossible.
If I get the job, I'll be really happy. = a real possibility
If I got the job, I'd be really happy. = very unlikely
I'll meet you later if I don't have to work late. = a real possibility
I'd meet you later if I didn't have to work late. = impossible

GRAMMAR PRACTICE

1 Match the two parts to make second conditional sentences.
1 If you had a daughter, _____
2 I would speak perfect English _____
3 Your computer wouldn't do strange things _____
4 If you told people about your website, _____
5 What would you do today _____
6 If I wrote a book, _____

a it would be much more popular.
b it would be about my childhood.
c if you weren't at work?
d if I came from the U.S.
e what would you name her?
f if it didn't have a virus.

2 Choose the correct form of the verbs to complete the conversation.

A What ¹*did / would* you do if your company ²*offered / would offer* you a job in Japan?
B If that happened, I ³*thought / 'd think* about it. If they ⁴*paid / would pay* me more money, I ⁵*'ll / 'd* probably go.
A But ⁶*wouldn't / didn't* you miss your family and friends if you went abroad?
B Yes, but they ⁷*can / could* visit me if I was in Japan. It ⁸*were / would be* a great opportunity if I went.
A I ⁹*wouldn't / didn't* go … not even if they ¹⁰*doubled / would double* my salary!

3 Complete the sentences with the verbs in parentheses so they are true for you. Use the second conditional if the situation is less likely. Use the first conditional if the situation is possible.

1 If it _____ (snow) this afternoon,
_____ .

2 If I _____ (pass) my English exam,
_____ .

3 If I _____ (see) my parents this evening,
_____ .

4 If my computer _____ (stop) working,
_____ .

5 If a reporter _____ (ask) me to appear on TV today,
_____ .

6 If I _____ (go) out with my friends after class,
_____ .

◀ Go back to page 53

VOCABULARY PRACTICE

1A Personality adjectives

1 ▶ 1.1 Match sentences 1–8 with pictures a–h. Listen and check.
  1 Rosa is very **shy**. She doesn't like talking to people she doesn't know. ____
  2 Michael is very **funny**. He makes the children laugh. ____
  3 Irene is very **patient**. She can wait for a long time and doesn't get angry. ____
  4 Marco always buys me coffee when we go out. He's really **generous**. ____
  5 Stefano is very **nice**. He's always happy to help me when I have a problem. ____
  6 Jane watches TV all day, and she never cleans the house. I think she's **lazy**. ____
  7 Arturo is very **polite**. He opens the door for us when we visit. ____
  8 Sita always tells the truth about everything. She's very **honest**. ____

2 A ▶ 1.2 Match the adjectives in the box below with the definitions in the chart. Listen and check.

| hard-working | sociable | dishonest | serious |
| rude | selfish | mean | impatient |

This type of person ...	adjective	opposite
1 only thinks about himself/herself.		
2 says and does things that hurt other people's feelings.		
3 works very hard.		
4 likes going out and meeting new people.		
5 doesn't like waiting for things.		
6 doesn't laugh very often.		
7 isn't very helpful to others.		
8 doesn't tell the truth.		

B Write the opposites of the adjectives in the right-hand column.

Look! We say *What is he/she like?* when we ask about personality.
What is your teacher like?   She's shy, but she's very nice.

3 Choose the correct adjectives to complete the sentences.
  1 Children can be very *impatient / mean / dishonest*. They can say very bad things and make each other cry.
  2 Paul prefers to be with people he knows. He's very *rude / patient / shy*.
  3 I think Leo's *dishonest / rude / lazy*. He plays computer games all day, and he doesn't do any work.
  4 Marco's very *selfish / impatient / lazy*. He drinks all the milk in the refrigerator and doesn't care about the rest of us.
  5 Amanda hates waiting for the bus. She's so *impatient / mean / selfish*.
  6 Anton is really *patient / generous / sociable* with his time and his money. He always buys me lunch when we get together.
  7 Artur doesn't smile or laugh very much, and he thinks a lot about things before making decisions. He's very *hard-working / polite / serious*.
  8 Sam's really *sociable / funny / nice*. He always makes us laugh when he tells us his stories.
  9 Stella is a *lazy / dishonest / serious* person. She lies to people so they think she's clever.
  10 Those children are very *polite / generous / honest*. If they break something, they always tell the teacher.

a

b

c

d

e

f

g

h

◀ Go back to page 4

VOCABULARY PRACTICE

1B Hobbies and socializing

1 1.7 Match the two columns in each group to make phrases. Listen and check.

Online activities

Socializing

1 download ___   a social media (e.g., Facebook)
2 go on ___   b about your opinions
3 blog ___   c music/movies/apps
4 play ___   d online
5 shop ___   e video games

11 spend ___   k a club
12 get together ___ l out at night
13 meet ___   m time with the family
14 join ___   n new people
15 go ___   o with friends

Sports and games

Other hobbies

6 stay ___   f soccer/chess
7 play ___   g Pilates
8 go ___   h in shape
9 do ___   i the gym/the swimming pool
10 go to ___   j running/swimming

16 bake ___   p at home
17 learn ___   q a concert/the movies
18 relax ___   r an instrument/a language
19 go to ___   s coins/records/stamps
20 collect ___   t a cake/cupcakes/bread

2 Complete the sentences with the correct forms of the verbs in the box.

| meet stay relax spend go join shop go on get together do |

1 It's important to _____ time with your friends and family.
2 Why don't you _____ a tennis club?
3 Karen usually _____ online because she is very busy.
4 I took an English course to _____ new people.
5 I think swimming is the best way to _____ in shape.
6 Ned doesn't have many hobbies. He just _____ at home.
7 I hardly ever _____ social media. I prefer meeting people face-to-face.
8 Saturday night is a good time to _____ with my friends.
9 You need to be in very good shape to _____ gymnastics.
10 Martin _____ running every morning at 6:00.

◀ Go back to page 6

137

VOCABULARY PRACTICE

1C Useful verbs

1 ▶ 1.15 Complete the sentences with the correct forms of the verbs. Listen and check.

1 **wear / carry**
It's a beautiful day. Why are you _____ an umbrella and _____ a coat?

2 **take / give**
Could you _____ me to the party, please? Brian says he can _____ me a ride home.

3 **look / look like**
A: She _____ beautiful in that dress, doesn't she?
B: Yes, she _____ her mother.

4 **look forward to / expect**
I'm _____ seeing my cousins again. We _____ their flight to arrive at any minute.

5 **say / tell**
Don't _____ her about the party. Charlotte _____ that she loves surprises!

6 **miss / lose**
Here are our movie tickets. Don't _____ them! I don't want to _____ the beginning of the movie.

7 **hope / wait**
I'm _____ for you at the restaurant. I _____ you're not going to be late.

8 **win / earn**
He doesn't _____ very much money as a writer, although he _____ a lot of competitions.

9 **remember / remind**
I have to _____ to buy some eggs. If I forget, can you please _____ me?

10 **go back / come back**
My parents are _____ from Greece today. They had a fantastic time. They want to _____ next year!

2 A Choose the correct verb to complete questions 1–8.

1 Who do you *look like / look* in your family?
2 Are you *going back / coming back* to college in the fall?
3 What did you *take / give* for lunch today?
4 How do you usually *wear / carry* your things to class?
5 Do you always *remember / remind* to do your homework?
6 Do you ever *lose / miss* your cell phone?
7 Do you always *say / tell* your parents the truth?
8 Where do you *hope / wait* to be in 10 years?

B Match questions 1–8 with answers a–h.

_____ a Yes. We start in October.
_____ b Nothing! I forgot my lunch at home.
_____ c I use a small backpack.
_____ d Sometimes, but I usually put it in my pocket.
_____ e Of course! I'm very honest.
_____ f I want to own my own company.
_____ g No, I don't. Sometimes I forget.
_____ h My mother. We have the same eyes.

◀ Go back to page 9

3B Vacation activities

1 ▶ 3.5 Complete the chart with the words in the box to make phrases. Listen and check.

> a museum   on a guided tour   abroad   a seat on a train   a resort
> local attractions   sightseeing   camping   a hotel   a flight   a double room

go	visit	stay at	reserve/book

2 ▶ 3.6 Match the sentences. Listen and check.

1 We always **sunbathe** on the beach. _____
2 I usually **buy souvenirs** for my family. _____
3 You can **rent a car** for a week. _____
4 On vacation, we usually **eat out** every night. _____
5 Let's **have a barbecue** on the weekend. _____
6 I sometimes **pack my suitcase** a week before we go. _____

a It's expensive, but we like to try the local food.
b The weather looks good.
c That way I don't forget anything.
d The local market is the best place to find presents.
e I like relaxing and listening to the ocean.
f It's a good way to see the countryside.

138

◀ Go back to page 24

VOCABULARY PRACTICE

2A -ed/-ing adjectives

1 ▶ 2.5 Look at the pictures and complete the sentences with the *-ed* or *-ing* adjectives. Listen and check.

1 **amazed / amazing**
The magic show was _____!
I was _____. The magician did some incredible tricks.

7 **annoyed / annoying**
I was _____ because Joe was playing loud music.
It's very _____ when people make a lot of noise.

2 **relaxed / relaxing**
I had a really _____ weekend.
I felt so _____ I took a nap on Saturday afternoon.

8 **disappointed / disappointing**
I failed my driving test last week. I was really _____.
It's _____, but I can take the test again.

3 **tired / tiring**
What a long day! I'm very _____ now.
It's _____ being a mother.

9 **excited / exciting**
I got my ticket for the music festival. I'm so _____!
It's always _____ to go to a live concert.

4 **interested / interesting**
I'm _____ in Roman history.
Do you have any _____ books on the subject?

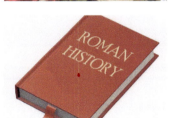

10 **terrified / terrifying**
I don't like this. I'm _____ of heights!
I didn't think cleaning windows would be so _____.

5 **bored / boring**
The class was very _____ this morning.
I was so _____, I fell asleep!

11 **confused / confusing**
These instructions are very _____.
I'm completely _____.
I don't know what this means.

6 **embarrassed / embarrassing**
I was _____ when the computer stopped working.
I couldn't give my presentation.
It was very _____.

12 **surprised / surprising**
Ana received a _____ e-mail this morning.
Ana was really _____ when she read the e-mail.

2 Choose the correct adjectives to complete the sentences.

1 The class was really *interested / interesting,* and all the students enjoyed it.
2 We were all *surprised / surprising* when we heard Katya's news.
3 The photos from the concert were really *disappointed / disappointing*.
4 Are you *excited / exciting* about moving abroad next year?
5 Horror movies are *terrified / terrifying*. I never watch them.
6 The exam questions were very *confused / confusing*. I didn't understand them at all.
7 I lost my phone, so I couldn't take any photos. It was very *annoyed / annoying*.
8 I was very *embarrassed / embarrassing* when I arrived late.

◀ Go back to page 13

139

VOCABULARY PRACTICE

2C Life stages

1 ▶ 2.6 Match the phrases in the box with the pictures on the timeline. Listen and check.

> be born   die   get engaged   graduate from college/high school   get your driver's license   go to elementary school   get a divorce
> fall in love   retire   get married   grow up   have children   finish school   go to middle school   start a career

2 Match the two columns to make sentences.

1 My grandmother was born _____
2 She grew up _____
3 She went to elementary school _____
4 She finished school when _____
5 She went to college _____
6 She started her career _____
7 There she met _____
8 They got married _____
9 They had two children— _____
10 My grandmother retired _____

a my grandfather, also a doctor.
b at the age of 65.
c she was 18, in 1961.
d my mother and my uncle.
e on April 14, 1961.
f in 1966, after getting engaged.
g when she was five.
h on a farm in Kentucky.
i as a doctor in a hospital.
j to study medicine.

3 Complete the text with the correct form of the life stages verbs.

1 My parents worked in lots of different countries, so I _____ with my grandparents in Miami.
2 Luca _____ to his girlfriend last week. The wedding is in May of next year.
3 I want to _____ in the summer. Then I can drive to college every day.
4 Sandra's parents _____ ten years ago, but they are still friends and see each other often.
5 Raul works in that hospital. He says almost 30 babies _____ there every day.

140

◀ Go back to page 16

VOCABULARY PRACTICE

3A Useful adjectives

1 ▶ 3.1 Match the adjectives in the box with the pictures 1–12. Listen and check.

> ancient   modern   crowded   famous   busy   lively   messy   polluted   quiet   ugly   uncomfortable   unusual

1 _____

2 _____

3 _____

4 _____

5 _____

6 _____

7 _____

8 _____

9 _____

10 _____

11 _____

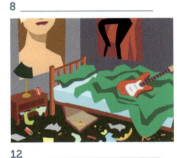
12 _____

2 Choose the correct word to complete the sentences.

1 Our hotel room was really *uncomfortable / quiet*. We complained to the manager.
2 Petra is one of the most *lively / famous* archaeological sites in the Middle East.
3 You will love this restaurant; it's always very *lively / crowded*.
4 We went to the beach for our vacation but the water was really *polluted / messy*.
5 It's impossible to get on the buses at rush hour because they are so *lively / crowded*.
6 If you go to Egypt, don't miss the *ugly / ancient* temples in Luxor and Aswan.
7 We loved Vietnam. The streets were really *busy / messy* with all kinds of vehicles and people.
8 He went all around the world and all he bought me was an *ugly / ancient* key ring.
9 We went for a walk away from downtown and found some *quiet / messy* streets.
10 We saw some very *unusual / uncomfortable* animals when we went to Australia.
11 There is a new building downtown; it's really *lively / modern*.
12 The children's rooms are always *unusual / messy* when they're on summer vacation.

3 Complete the text with the correct adjectives.

> My first trip to a foreign country was in 2015, when I visited Cambodia. My favorite place was Angkor Wat, which is one of the most ¹_____ archaeological sites in the world. There are hundreds of ²_____ temples from the 12th century in an area of over 1 km²! It's a very ³_____ place, but I'm very glad I went.
>
> I went very early in the morning because it gets very ⁴_____ later in the day, and the buses get ⁵_____ . You can visit the site by yourself, or hire a guide who can show you around and explain everything. Remember not to wear ⁶_____ shoes, because you have to walk a lot!

◀ Go back to page 22

VOCABULARY PRACTICE

4A Jobs

1 ▶ 4.1 Match the words in the box with the pictures 1–12. Listen and check.

> lawyer accountant waiter/waitress receptionist surgeon firefighter
> scientist hairdresser journalist model salesperson farmer

1 _____

2 _____

3 _____

4 _____

5 _____

6 _____

7 _____

8 _____

9 _____

10 _____

11 _____

12 _____

2 ▶ 4.2 Match the words to make jobs. Listen and check.

1 fashion _____   a guide
2 movie _____   b designer
3 soccer _____   c officer
4 police _____   d coach
5 security _____ e reporter
6 sales _____   f guard
7 tour _____   g person
8 news _____   h director
9 travel _____   i attendant
10 flight _____   j agent

3 Complete the sentences with the correct jobs from exercises 1 and 2.

1 Whenever I have my hair cut, I always tell the _____ all my problems.
2 I didn't know where to go on vacation, but the _____ suggested some good places.
3 I was worried about the operation, but the _____ said everything would be fine.
4 I went to buy a new shirt and the _____ was very helpful.
5 The _____ might lose his job. The team has lost ten games now!
6 Why don't you speak to a _____ before you sign this contract?
7 My mother is a _____ . She works for a company that develops new medicines.
8 Our plane was full, but the _____ was very helpful.
9 The concert was really crowded, and a _____ said I couldn't go in.
10 I'm sure the company has financial problems. The _____ looks very worried!

◀ Go back to page 30

VOCABULARY PRACTICE

4C Phrases about work

1 ▶ 4.11 Match the phrases with the pictures. Listen and check.

> agree on a salary   apply for a job   get a job offer
> get a pay raise   get a promotion   have an interview
> quit a job   see a job ad   start work   write a résumé

2 Complete the sentences with the correct form of the verbs from exercise 1.

1 I would like to _____ for the job of assistant manager.
2 I'm very bored at work. I'm going to _____ my job.
3 My husband _____ a pay raise last week, so we're going to buy an apartment.
4 It looks like a fabulous new job. When do you _____ work?
5 I _____ a job ad in the paper last week. It looks really interesting!
6 My sister _____ a promotion. Now she is the director. We're all very proud of her.
7 All the new jobs will be advertised next month. I need to _____ a résumé.
8 I _____ three job offers in one week! I'm not sure what to do!
9 She can't go to the meeting on Tuesday. She _____ an interview for a new job.
10 The interview went well and I want the job, but we can't _____ a salary.

3 ▶ 4.12 Match 1–8 with a–h to make expressions. Listen and check.

1 see ____   a interested in a career in …
2 send ____   b a degree in …
3 have ____   c a training course
4 take ____   d for an interview at any time
5 be ____   e for a salary between …
6 look ____   f as an intern
7 go ____   g a résumé, an application form
8 work ____   h an advertisement, an ad

4 Complete the letter with the words in the box.

> degree   interview   advertisement   salary   application   career

Dear Sir/Madam:

I saw your ¹_____ for the job of Software Engineer, and I'd like to apply. I am sending you my résumé and an ²_____ form.

I have a ³_____ in Information Technology, and I am very interested in a ⁴_____ in software development. I am looking for a ⁵_____ of between $30,000 and $35,000 and I can go for an ⁶_____ at any time during the next two weeks.

I look forward to hearing from you.

Best regards,

Chloe Maxwell

1 _____

2 _____

3 _____

4 _____

5 _____

6 _____

7 _____

8 _____

9 _____

10 _____

◀ Go back to page 35

143

VOCABULARY PRACTICE

5A Health and medicine

1 ▶ 5.1 Complete the problems 1–16 with the words in the box. Listen and check.

| stomachache | backache | broke | nosebleed | burned | cold | cough | cut |
| earache | flu | headache | hurts | sore throat | stressed | temperature | toothache |

1 I _____ my hand.

2 I have a _____ .

3 I _____ my finger.

4 I _____ my leg.

5 I have a _____ .

6 I have a _____ .

7 I have a _____ .

8 I have a _____ .

9 I have a _____ .

10 I have an _____ .

11 I have a _____ .

12 I have a _____ .

13 I'm _____ .

14 My knee _____ .

15 I have the _____ .

16 I have a _____ .

2 Match problems 1–9 with possible solutions in the box. There may be more than one answer.

1 I don't feel well. I have a stomachache. _____
2 Those boxes were heavy. I have a backache now! _____
3 Ooh! I have a sore throat. _____
4 I'm worried about my nosebleeds. _____
5 I have a terrible headache. _____
6 I feel awful. I think I have the flu. _____
7 I'm stressed about work. _____
8 I burned my hand yesterday. It still hurts. _____
9 My foot hurts. I fell getting out of the car! _____

see a doctor   call a friend
take some pills   put some ice / cold water on it
rest in bed   have some hot lemon and honey
go lie down   talk to your boss
have some chicken soup   put some cream on it
go to bed early every night   eat healthy food

◀ Go back to page 40

VOCABULARY PRACTICE

5B Collocations with *do*, *make*, *have*, and *take*

1 ▶ 5.5 Complete the diagrams with *do*, *make*, *have*, or *take*. Listen and check.

2 Complete the sentences with the correct form of the verbs *do*, *make*, *have*, or *take*.

1 I _____ a bad argument with my parents last night.
2 Alvin always finishes his work late and _____ an excuse.
3 If you want to make good sushi, you have to _____ your time.
4 Don't _____ any mistakes or you'll have to start over.
5 To relax, she _____ Pilates every day after work.
6 We _____ a great time when we went to California.
7 Lisa _____ her best, but she failed the exam.
8 I don't have a reservation, but I'm going to _____ a chance and go.

◀ Go back to page 42

6A Phrasal verbs

1 ▶ 6.1 Match sentences 1–8 with the pictures a–h. Listen and check.

1 Can I **turn on** the air-conditioning? ____
2 I'm going to **find out** who did this. ____
3 Oh no! We've **run out of** milk! ____
4 Why did the car **break down** here? ____
5 Please **throw away** the empty bottles. ____
6 Can you **fill up** the car with gasoline, please? ____
7 You should **clean up** your bedroom. ____
8 I'm going to **look up** the word in a dictionary. ____

2 ▶ 6.2 Match the phrasal verbs in **bold** with their meanings a–h. Listen and check.

1 I don't want to **go on** with the course. It's boring.   a wait
2 If you want to get in shape you should **take up** running. b continue
3 I'm going to **take care of** my sister's children tonight. c stop
4 You need to **fill out** this form to get a passport. d start
5 Can you **give back** the money you owe me? e return
6 You should **give up** smoking. It's bad for you. f be with
7 If you **hold on** for five minutes, I'll come, too. g complete
8 The snow will soon **turn into** water. h become

3 Complete the sentences with the correct form of the phrasal verbs.

1 My car is awful. It _____ every month!
2 Yesterday, I _____ that I'm going to get a pay raise.
3 I'm going to _____ this pen. It's broken.
4 It rained at first, but then it _____ a beautiful day.
5 Two years ago, Colin _____ milk for health reasons.
6 The store _____ size 8 jeans yesterday.
7 Can you _____ my cat while I'm away on vacation?
8 I'm on my way! Please, _____ for another five minutes.

◀ Go back to page 48

145

VOCABULARY PRACTICE

5C Emotions and feelings

1 ▶ 5.10 Look at the pictures. Match sentences 1–12 with people a–l. Listen and check.

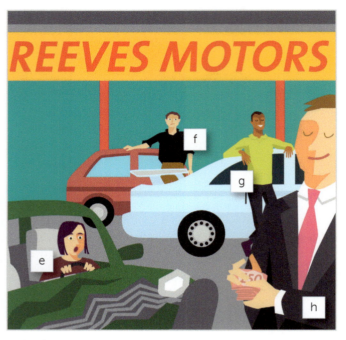

1 Roberto feels very **confident**. He thinks he'll get the job. ____
2 Mr. Wallace doesn't like his job. He looks **miserable**. ____
3 Karen isn't worried about the interview. She's very **calm** today. ____
4 Peter hates interviews. He gets very **nervous**. ____

5 Kevin's very **proud** of his expensive new car. ____
6 Joe's **envious** of Kevin's car. He can't afford a new one. ____
7 Mr. Reeves has made a lot of money. He's **delighted**. ____
8 Sally's very **upset** because she had a car accident. ____

2 Choose the correct words to complete the sentences.

1 I studied really hard for this exam. I'm *proud / confident / delighted* I will pass.
2 Claire's really *calm / guilty / upset* because her boss invited everyone to a party except her.
3 Patrick borrowed his neighbor's coffeemaker and broke it. He feels really *guilty / envious / miserable*.
4 I was *cheerful / delighted / confident* when I got a pay raise and a promotion at work.
5 I moved to the city last year. I see lots of people, but I still feel *envious / confident / lonely* sometimes.
6 My son won a writing competition. I'm very *proud / confident / delighted* of him.
7 My neighbor finishes work at 2:00 p.m. every day. I sometimes feel really *upset / envious / guilty* of her!
8 When she listens to classical music, she always feels very *cheerful / confident / calm*.
9 Jo doesn't like public speaking, but she's going to give a presentation this afternoon. She's really *lonely / nervous / upset*.
10 I feel *miserable / jealous / guilty*. My train was late, I lost my phone, and now it's starting to rain!
11 Malika's son is only 3 years old. He gets *guilty / lonely / jealous* when she plays with her friends' children.
12 My boss was very *cheerful / delighted / proud* today. She was singing a song when she came into the office.

9 Vikram loves his job. He's very **cheerful** today. ____
10 Lucia forgot Jess's birthday, and is one hour late. She feels **guilty**. ____
11 Jess is celebrating her birthday by herself. She feels very **lonely**. ____
12 Mr. Lee's **jealous**. He doesn't like his wife talking to Vincent. ____

◀ Go back to page 44

VOCABULARY PRACTICE

6C The natural world

1A Match the landscapes in the box with pictures 1–3.

mountains   rainforest   coast

B ▶ 6.7 Match the words with the natural features a–r. Listen and check.

river ____
stream ____
rocks ____
branch ____
roots ____
wildlife ____

cliff ____
ocean ____
waves ____
shore ____
lightning ____
thunderstorm ____

cave ____
peak ____
valley ____
waterfall ____
lake ____
sunrise/sunset ____

2 ~~Cross out~~ the word that is incorrect in each sentence.
1 I took a photo of the *sunset / sunrise / roots* because the sky was so pink.
2 We saw a snake sitting on a *branch / rock / stream*.
3 You can drink the water from *the ocean / a river / a stream*.
4 You can hear the *cave / thunder / waterfall* from a long way away.
5 He believes there are bears living in the *root / cave / valley*.
6 My feet got wet while I was walking along the *lake / shore / wildlife*.
7 She wants to climb up this *cliff / peak / wave*, but it's very difficult.
8 We didn't expect to see a *thunderstorm / ocean / wildlife* on our trip to the mountains.

3 Complete the sentences with words a–h.
1 One of the driest places in the world is Death ____.   a River
2 In Acapulco, people dive into the ocean from high ____.   b coast
3 Cairo is on the banks of the Nile ____.   c lake
4 Niagara is an amazing ____ in the U.S. and Canada.   d lightning
5 Every year, we drive along the Atlantic ____.   e cliffs
6 Surfers love going to Hawaii for its giant ____.   f Valley
7 In 1963, a plane crashed when ____ hit it.   g waves
8 They say the Loch Ness Monster lives in a ____   h waterfall
  in Scotland.

◀ Go back to page 52

147

COMMUNICATION PRACTICE

1A Student A

1 Look at the activities and ask Student B questions with *How often ... ?* Write down his/her answers.

   1 see the dentist   _____
   2 go to the movies   _____
   3 buy clothes   _____
   4 check your phone   _____
   5 exercise   _____
   6 eat in a restaurant   _____

2 Answer Student B's questions using adverbs and expressions of frequency.

> always   usually   sometimes   often   hardly ever   never
> once/twice/three times a day/week/month
> every day/week/month

3 Tell the class what you found out about your partner.

1C Student A

1 Look at pictures 1–4. Ask Student B questions to guess what is happening.

   A *Is the woman in picture 1 going for a walk?*   B *No, she isn't.*

2 Answer Student B's questions about pictures 5–8.

2A Student A

1 Ask Student B *What did you do ... ?* with the time expressions. Add the correct prepositions, if necessary.

   A *What did you do in the summer?*
   B *I studied for my exams, but I got together with friends, too.*

> the summer   yesterday   8:00 this morning   last week   2015   two weeks ago

2 Answer Student B's questions.

2D Student A

1 Read sentences 1–5 to Student B and listen to his/her responses.

   1 I fell down last week and broke my arm.
   2 I got a new car for my birthday.
   3 My brother found a wallet with $100 in it.
   4 Yesterday was the best day ever!
   5 I met someone famous yesterday.

2 Listen to Student B's sentences and respond to show you are interested.

   B *I didn't get home from work until 10:00 p.m. last night.*
   A *You poor thing! What happened?*

COMMUNICATION PRACTICE

2C Student A

1 Ask Student B questions about your mystery person and complete the chart. Can you guess who she is?

When / born?		1935
Where / grow up?		Mississippi, U.S.
What / first job after finishing school?		Salesperson
How many times / get married?		Once–to Priscilla
Have / children?		Yes, a daughter named Lisa Marie
How / become famous?		Made lots of records, including "Jailhouse Rock" and "Can't Help Falling in Love"
When / die?		1977

2 Answer your partner's questions about Elvis Presley. Remember, don't use his name! Can Student B guess who he is?

3A Student A

1 Complete the sentences with the superlative form of the adjectives in parentheses and guess the answer. Student B will say if you are correct.

1 The _____ animals in the world are … (*dangerous*)

crocodiles   sharks   snakes

3 The _____ car in the world is … (*fast*)

Porsche 959   McLaren F1   Bugatti Veyron

2 The _____ sports event was … (*popular*)

Brazil World Cup, 2014   Beijing Olympics, 2008   Superbowl XLVI, 2012

4 The _____ place in the world is … (*noisy*)

Times Square, New York   Champs Élysées, Paris   Exchange Square, Hong Kong

2 Listen to Student B's sentences. Look at the information and say if he/she is correct. Give more information using comparatives, superlatives, and *(not) as … as*.

The Amazon isn't as long as the Nile, but it's longer than the Yangtze.

1 The Nile (6,853 km.); the Amazon (6,437 km.); the Yangtze (6,300 km.)
2 *Nafea Faa Ipoipo*, Paul Gauguin ($300 million); *The Card Players*, Paul Cézanne ($274 million); *The Grand Canal*, Claude Monet ($35 million)
3 Manila, the Philippines (41,014 people/km.^{2}); Cairo, Egypt (36,618 people/km.^{2}); Buenos Aires, Argentina (13,680 people/km.^{2})
4 The Beatles (265 million albums); Michael Jackson (175 million albums); Madonna (166 million albums)

4D Student A

1 You call a company to rent a car for one week. Call Student B and use the details below. Speak as quickly as possible!

Name: George Graddoll
Car: 5-door Subaru Impreza
Dates: Monday, March 1 (12:00)–Sunday, March 7 (18:00)
Credit card: Visa - CD25 5221 BZ55 Xy23

2 You work in a restaurant. Student B will call to reserve a table for tonight. Ask him/her questions and complete the form as accurately as possible.

Customer name: _____
Telephone number: _____
Number of people: _____
Time: _____
Special requirements: _____

159

COMMUNICATION PRACTICE

3C Student A

1   Read the text about Harold Bride. Prepare questions for Student B. Use the answers to complete the story.

   1 What / Harold Bride's job?
   2 What / he / do / on April 14, at 11:40 p.m.?
   3 What / Captain Edward Smith / say?
   4 What / water / force into the ocean?
   5 What / he / send from the radio room?

2   Answer Student B's questions to help him/her complete the story.

THE STORY OF A SURVIVOR

Harold Bride was working on the *Titanic* when the ship sank over 100 years ago. He was a ¹_____ who sent and received important information. He was on board when the ship began its voyage from Southampton on April 10, 1912.

On April 14, at 11:40 p.m., Bride ²_____ in his room when he heard a terrible noise. He woke up and went straight to the radio room to find out what was happening. Just after midnight, Captain Edward Smith came in and said that ³_____ . He asked Bride to send an emergency signal to any other ships in the area. The nearest ship to respond was the *Carpathia*, but, unfortunately, it didn't arrive until after the *Titanic* sank.

While the *Titanic* was filling up with water, Bride continued to send messages. However, the equipment eventually stopped working, and Bride went to help release one of the last lifeboats. But the water forced the ⁴_____ into the freezing ocean.

Bride held onto the damaged lifeboat and, after hours in the water, some sailors rescued him and took him onto the *Carpathia*. He was badly hurt, so he rested for a while, but later he went to the radio room and began to send ⁵_____ .

4A Student A

1 Ask Student B questions with *will*. Check (✓) his/her answers in the chart.

Do you think ...	likely	possible	unlikely	impossible
you will move in the next five years?				
you will get a (new) job soon?				
you will become famous?				
you will live abroad in the future?				
you will learn to speak English fluently?				
you will do anything exciting this week?				

2 Answer Student B's questions using the phrases in the box. Give more information.

   B *Do you think you will go on vacation next summer?*
   A *Yes, I think I will. I'll probably visit my family in Miami.*

   Yes, I think I will.   Yes, I probably will.
   Yes, I may.   Yes, I might.
   I don't think I will.   I probably won't.
   I definitely won't.

4C Student A

1 Student B has applied for a job in your company. You call him/her to set up an interview. Look at your day planner and find a time to schedule the interview.

   B *I'm free on Monday afternoon. Can we have the interview then?*
   A *I'm sorry, I'm meeting with the marketing team. What about Monday morning?*

Monday	morning	
	afternoon	meet with the Marketing team
Tuesday	morning	
	afternoon	visit the factory
Wednesday	morning	
	afternoon	meet with the managing director
Thursday	morning	
	afternoon	
Friday	morning	fly to Paris
	afternoon	have lunch with Peter

COMMUNICATION PRACTICE

5A Student A

1 Tell Student B about your problems and write down the advice that he/she gives you.

Your problems	Advice
I can't sleep at night.	
I burned my hand while I was cooking.	
I have a bad headache.	
I have a nosebleed.	
I want to lose weight.	

2 Student B will tell you about a problem. Give him/her some advice using the ideas from the box and your own ideas.

get some exercise	drink so much coffee	eat junk food
eat more fruit	go to bed	go to the hospital
go to work today	lie down	lose some weight
put a bandage on it	work so hard	put some cream on it
rest	see a doctor	talk to a friend
stay at home	take the day off work	

*You should ...   I think you should ...   You shouldn't ...
I don't think you should ...*

5C Student A

1 Read the beginnings of sentences 1–6 to Student B. He/She will complete the sentences.

  1 If I don't feel well tomorrow morning ...
  2 If it snows this weekend ...
  3 If I'm invited to a costume party ...
  4 If I don't have any homework tonight ...
  5 If I have to cook dinner tonight ...
  6 If I'm stressed at work ...

2 Listen to the beginnings of the sentences Student B reads to you. Choose the correct ending to complete the sentence and tell him/her.

... I might have a party to celebrate.
... I probably won't get a dog.
... I'll buy some new jeans.
... I'll take an aspirin.
... I might go to Cuba.
... I might get a promotion.

6A Student A

1 Complete the *Have you ever ...?* questions with the past participles of the verbs in parentheses and ask Student B. He/She will always answer with *Yes, I have.* Ask him/her the simple past questions and decide if he/she is telling the truth.

2 Student B will ask you a *Have you ever ...?* question. You should always answer with *Yes, I have.* He/She will ask you more questions. If it is true, tell the truth. If it is not true, invent the details.

	Have you ever ...	Simple past
1	_____ on TV? (be)	What show were you on? What did you do? Did many people watch the show?
2	_____ something valuable by mistake? (throw away)	What was it? How much was it worth? Did you find it again?
3	_____ karaoke? (sing)	When did you sing karaoke? Which song did you sing? Did you sing it well?
4	_____ something and not given it back? (borrow)	What did you borrow? Who lent it to you? Were they angry about it?
5	_____ a dangerous animal? (take care of)	What kind of animal was it? Why did you have to take care of it? Did you have any problems?

6C Student A

1 Complete the sentences with the correct form of the verbs in parentheses. Decide if the sentence is true or false for you. Read your sentences to Student B.

  1 If I _____ near the ocean, I _____ swimming every day. (live / go)
  2 I _____ a friend $50 if he/she _____ to borrow it. (not lend / ask)
  3 If someone _____ to steal my bike, I _____ them. (try / stop)
  4 I _____ terrified if my friends _____ me to go mountain climbing. (be / ask)
  5 If I _____ outside in a thunderstorm, I _____ under a tree. (be / hide)

2 Listen to Student B's sentences. Decide if they are true or false. He/She will tell you if you are correct.

  B *If I had more money, I'd buy a new car.*
  A *False.*
  B *Yes, you're right. If I had more money, I'd go on vacation.*

161

COMMUNICATION PRACTICE

1A Student B

1 Answer Student A's questions using the frequency adverbs and expressions.

> always usually sometimes often hardly ever never
> once/twice/three times a day/week/month
> every day/week/month

2 Tell the class what you found out about your partner.

3 Look at the activities and ask Student A questions with *How often ... ?* Write down his/her answers.

1 download music _____
2 send an e-mail _____
3 get angry _____
4 cook dinner _____
5 read a newspaper _____
6 dance _____

1C Student B

1 Answer Student A's questions about pictures 1–4.

A *Is the woman in picture 5 going for a walk?* B *No, she isn't.*

2 Look at pictures 5–8. Ask Student A questions to guess what is happening.

2A Student B

1 Answer Student A's questions.

2 Ask Student A *What did you do ... ?* with the time expressions. Add the correct prepositions, if necessary.

> December 31 an hour ago the weekend February Friday night last month

B *What did you do last year on December 31?*
A *I went to a street party with my friends and danced until midnight.*

2D Student B

1 Listen to Student A's sentences and respond to show you are interested.

A *I didn't get home from work until 10:00 p.m. last night.*
B *You poor thing! What happened?*

2 Read sentences 1–5 to Student A and listen to his/her responses.

1 I have a new job.
2 My car didn't start this morning.
3 My sister wants to get married on a beach next year.
4 I had a terrible day yesterday.
5 I won a trip to India in a contest.

COMMUNICATION PRACTICE

2C Student B

1 Answer your partner's questions about Marilyn Monroe. Remember, don't use her name! Can Student A guess who she is?

When / born?	1926
Where / grow up?	California, U.S.
What / first job after finishing school?	Factory worker
How many times / get married?	Three times–to James Dougherty, Joe DiMaggio, and Arthur Miller
Have / children?	No
How / become famous?	She made lots of movies, including *Gentlemen Prefer Blondes* and *How to Marry a Millionaire*
When / die?	1962

2 Ask Student A questions about your mystery person and complete the chart. Can you guess who he is?

3A Student B

1 Listen to Student A's sentences. Look at the information and say if he/she is correct. Give more information using comparatives, superlatives, and *(not) as … as*.

Crocodiles aren't as dangerous as snakes, but they're more dangerous than sharks.

1 snakes (50,000 deaths/year); crocodiles (10,000 deaths/year); sharks (20 deaths/year)
2 Brazil World Cup, 2014 (700 million viewers); Beijing Olympics, 2008 (600 million viewers); Superbowl XLVI, 2012 (110 million viewers)
3 Bugatti Veyron (415 km./h); McLaren F1 (408 km./h); Porsche 959 (317 km./h)
4 Times Square, New York (80 decibels); Champs Élysées, Paris (79 decibels); Exchange Square, Hong Kong (78 decibels)

2 Complete the sentences with the superlative form of the adjectives in parentheses and guess the answer. Student A will say if you are correct.

1 The _____ river in the world is … (*long*)

  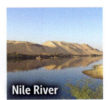

Amazon River Yangtze River Nile River

3 The _____ city in the world is … (*crowded*)

Buenos Aires, Argentina Manila, The Philippines Cairo, Egypt

2 The _____ painting ever sold is … (*expensive*)

The Grand Canal, Claude Monet *Nafea Faa Ipoipo*, Paul Gauguin *The Card Players*, Paul Cézanne

4 The _____ musical artist is … (*successful*)

Madonna Michael Jackson The Beatles

4D Student B

1 You work for a rental car company. Student A will call to rent a car. Ask him/her questions and complete the form as accurately as possible.

Customer name: _____
Credit card: _____
Type of car: _____
Pick up date and time: _____
Number of days: _____

2 You call a restaurant to reserve a table for tonight. Call Student A and use the details below. Speak as quickly as possible!

Name: Lysandra Apostolakis
Phone number: 202-555-0110
Time: 7:00 (but may be late)
People: 8 adults, 4 children, 1 baby (need highchair for baby)

167

COMMUNICATION PRACTICE

3C Student B

1. Read the text about Harold Bride. Answer Student A's questions to help him/her complete the story.

2. Make questions for Student A. Use the answers to complete the story.
   1. When / the *Titanic* / begin / its voyage?
   2. Why / he / go / to the radio room?
   3. What / name of the nearest ship?
   4. What / happen / while / Bride / send / the messages?
   5. What / Bride / hold onto / in the water?

THE STORY OF A SURVIVOR

Harold Bride was working on the *Titanic* when the ship sank over 100 years ago. He was a radio operator who sent and received important information. He was on board when the ship began its voyage from Southampton on [1]_____.

On April 14 at 11:40 p.m., Bride was sleeping in his room when he heard a terrible noise. He woke up and went straight to the radio room to [2]_____. Just after midnight, Captain Edward Smith came in and said that the ship was sinking. He asked Bride to send an emergency signal to any other ships in the area. The nearest ship to respond was [3]_____, but, unfortunately, it didn't arrive until after the *Titanic* sank. While the [4]_____, Bride continued to send messages. However, the equipment eventually stopped working and Bride went to help release one of the last lifeboats. But the water forced the lifeboat and the men into the freezing ocean.

Bride held onto the [5]_____ and, after hours in the water, some sailors rescued him and took him onto the *Carpathia*. He was badly hurt so he rested for a while, but later he went to the radio room and began to send personal messages from the survivors.

4A Student B

1. Answer Student A's questions using the phrases in the box. Give more information.

   > Yes, I think I will.   Yes, I probably will.
   > Yes, I may.   Yes, I might.
   > I don't think I will.   I probably won't.
   > I definitely won't.

   A *Do you think you will move in the next five years?*
   B *Yes, I might. My downtown apartment is very small, and I want to look for a bigger one.*

2. Ask Student A questions with *will*. Check (✓) his/her answers in the chart.

Do you think ...	likely	possible	unlikely	impossible
you will go on vacation next summer?				
you will travel abroad this year?				
you will make any new friends this month?				
you will earn a lot of money in your next job?				
you will live to be 100 years old?				
you will eat in a restaurant next week?				

4C Student B

1. You applied for a job at Student A's company. He/She calls you to set up an interview. Look at your day planner and find a time to have the interview.

   A *I'm free on Monday morning. Can we have the interview then?*
   B *I'm sorry, I'm visiting my aunt in the hospital. What about Monday afternoon?*

Monday	morning	visit Aunt Emma in the hospital
	afternoon	
Tuesday	morning	see the dentist at 10:00
	afternoon	
Wednesday	morning	
	afternoon	go to Jenny's birthday lunch
Thursday	morning	take piano class
	afternoon	
Friday	morning	
	afternoon	play the piano at the jazz concert

COMMUNICATION PRACTICE

5A Student B

1 Student A will tell you about a problem. Give him/her some advice using the ideas from the box and your own ideas.

drink lots of water	drink so much coffee
eat so much chocolate	go on a diet
go to bed early	go to the pharmacy
go to the hospital	go to work today
hold it under cold water	hold your nose with a tissue
join a gym	move around too much
see a doctor	put some cream on it
take some pills	sit down for a few minutes
smoke	take some medicine

You should ...   I think you should ...
You shouldn't ...   I don't think you should ...

2 Tell Student A about your problems and write down the advice that he/she gives you.

Your problems	Advice
I feel tired all the time.	
I cut my hand on a piece of glass.	
I have a backache.	
I'm stressed.	
I have a stomachache.	

5C Student B

1 Listen to the beginnings of the sentences Student A reads to you. Choose the correct ending to complete the sentence and tell him/her.

... I won't make pasta.
... I might go as Superman.
... I'll probably watch a movie.
... I'll speak to my boss.
... I'll stay in bed.
... I might go skiing.

2 Read the beginnings of sentences 1–6 to Student A. He/She will complete the sentences.

1 If I go on vacation this summer ...
2 If I decide to get a pet ...
3 If my boss thinks I'm doing a good job ...
4 If I pass my exams ...
5 If I have a headache ...
6 If I go shopping on the weekend ...

6A Student B

1 Student A will ask you a *Have you ever ...?* question. You should always answer with *Yes, I have*. He/She will ask you more questions. If it is true, tell the truth. If it is not true, invent the details.

2 Complete the *Have you ever ...?* questions with the past participles of the verbs in parentheses and ask Student A. He/She will always answer with *Yes, I have*. Ask him/her the simple past questions and decide if he/she is telling the truth.

	Have you ever ...	Simple past
1	_____ an e-mail in English? (write)	When did you write it? Who did you send it to? Did you have any problems?
2	_____ all night to see the sunrise? (stay up)	Why didn't you sleep? How did you feel? What was it like?
3	_____ London? (visit)	When did you go there? Did you have a good time? What things did you see there?
4	_____ money your trip? (run out of)	Where did you go? Did you have any problems? How did you get more money?
5	_____ your house keys? (lose)	How did you get into your house? Do you know where you lost the keys? Did you find them again?

6C Student B

1 Listen to Student A's sentences. Decide if they are true or false. He/She will tell you if you are correct.

A *If I had more money, I'd buy a new car.*
B *False.*
A *Yes, you're right. If I had more money,*
　　I'd go on vacation.

2 Complete the sentences with the correct form of the verbs in parentheses. Decide if the sentence is true or false for you. Read your sentences to Student A.

1 I _____ my friends if I _____ my driving test. (not tell / fail)
2 If I _____ a spider in the bathtub, I _____ and take it outside. (find / pick it up)
3 If I _____ a lot of money, I _____ it with my friends. (win / share)
4 I _____ an animal to eat if I _____ any other food. (kill / not have)
5 If I _____ , I _____ more free time. (not work / have)

COMMUNICATION PRACTICE

6D All students

1 You're going on a trip to a rainforest for one week. You can only take six of the items with you. Decide which are the most useful.

tent   mosquito net   flashlight   first-aid kit   water-purifying kit   sunscreen

knife   food   compass and maps   insect repellent   cooking equipment   rope

2 In groups of four, discuss which six items you will take. Try to take turns politely.

3A Quiz results

For each answer A, score 0 points. For each answer B, score 1 point.

0–1 points = tourist. You're happiest sunbathing on a beach.
2–3 points = traveler. You like to do something more unusual on vacation.
4–5 points = adventurer. The best vacation for you is six months in the jungle!

5C Quiz results

For each answer A, score 0 points. For each answer B, score 1 point. For each answer C, score 2 points. For each answer D, score 3 points.

0–3 = Oh dear, you're really miserable right now. Are you upset about something? If you talk to your friends or family, you'll feel better.
4–7 = You're not very happy right now. If you do something you enjoy, maybe you'll feel more cheerful.
8–11 = Great news, you're happy! If you're friendly and smile at everyone today, you'll make them feel happier, too!
12–15 = You're extremely happy! Are you delighted about something? What's the secret to feeling so happy?

6C Quiz results

How many answers did you get right?

0–1 = You probably wouldn't survive if you went on a weekend camping trip. It's safer for you to stay at home.
2–3 = If you were in a difficult situation, you'd probably survive, but don't take any risks. Always find out about the dangers of a place before you go.
4 = Wow! You'd know what to do if you were in the wild. If you could choose an exciting place for an adventure, where would you go?

6D Quiz results

How many times did you answer yes?

0–2 = You don't like taking risks. Be careful, if you always play it safe, you might miss out on opportunities in your life.
3–4 = You're happy to take a risk, but not too many. That's probably the best way to be.
5–6 = You're a real risk-taker! It can be exciting, but watch out, it can be dangerous, too!

IRREGULAR VERBS

Infinitive	Simple past	Past participle
be	was, were	been
become	became	become
begin	began	begun
bite	bit	bitten
break	broke	broken
bring	brought	brought
build	built	built
buy	bought	bought
choose	chose	chosen
come	came	come
cost	cost	cost
do	did	done
dream	dreamed/dreamt	dreamed/dreamt
forbid	forbade	forbidden
forget	forgot	forgotten
forgive	forgave	forgiven
get	got	gotten
give	gave	given
go	went	gone
grow	grew	grown
have	had	had
hear	heard	heard
hide	hid	hidden
hold	held	held
keep	kept	kept
know	knew	known
learn	learned	learned
leave	left	left
let	let	let
lose	lost	lost

Infinitive	Simple past	Past participle
make	made	made
meet	met	met
pay	paid	paid
put	put	put
read (/rid/)	read (/red/)	read (/red/)
ride	rode	ridden
ring	rang	rung
rise	rose	risen
run	ran	run
say	said	said
see	saw	seen
sell	sold	sold
send	sent	sent
sleep	slept	slept
speak	spoke	spoken
spend	spent	spent
stand	stood	stood
steal	stole	stolen
stick	stuck	stuck
swim	swam	swum
take	took	taken
teach	taught	taught
tell	told	told
think	thought	thought
throw	threw	thrown
understand	understood	understood
wake	woke	woken
wear	wore	worn
win	won	won
write	wrote	written

American English

Personal Best

Workbook **B1** Pre-intermediate

UNIT 1 All about me

GRAMMAR: Simple present and adverbs of frequency

1 Order the words to complete the sentences.

1. gets together with / her friend Pat / sometimes
   Gloria _____ for coffee.
2. hardly ever / the bus / takes
   Daniel _____ to work.
3. ride your bike / you / often
   Do _____ to the office?
4. never / any / does
   Miguel _____ housework.
5. listen / to / often
   We _____ the radio.
6. visit / always / my friend
   I _____ on the weekend.
7. see / she / does / often
   How _____ Mario?
8. study / usually / don't
   They _____ in the morning.
9. to / sometimes / goes
   Silvia _____ the theater.
10. usually / eat / doesn't
    Alicia _____ breakfast.

2 Complete the sentences with the correct form of the verbs in parentheses.

1. Greta _____ two brothers. (have)
2. Peter _____ his hair every day. (wash)
3. My friend Enrique _____ in a factory. (work)
4. Marta and Luis _____ in Buenos Aires; they live in Brasília. (not live)
5. _____ you _____ Portuguese? (speak)
6. Ben _____ to Europe every summer to visit his family. (fly)
7. We _____ swimming. (not like)
8. _____ they _____ to the same school as you? (go)

VOCABULARY: Personality adjectives

3 Match descriptions 1–8 with adjectives a–h.

1. Anna often says things that upset other people. _____
2. Ed's always buying presents for his friends. _____
3. Pablo hardly ever laughs. _____
4. Terri doesn't like meeting new people. _____
5. The children always remember to say "please" and "thank you." _____
6. George tells lies and tricks people. _____
7. Dad goes to the office on weekends! _____
8. My math teacher explains things carefully and never gets angry. _____

a serious
b hard-working
c shy
d dishonest
e polite
f mean
g patient
h generous

4 Complete the adjectives. The first letters are given.

1. My brother is a really im_____ person; he hates standing in line to pay.
2. Lola is so se_____ that she only thinks about herself.
3. You can believe everything that Julia tells you; she's a very ho_____ person.
4. Ricardo never says hello to my parents when he comes to our house. They think he's r_____.
5. Marc is very so_____; he has lots of friends and often has parties at his house.
6. Hannah is so f_____; I never stop laughing when I'm with her.
7. Dan often helps me with jobs I need to do. He's very n_____.
8. Maria's so l_____; she stays in bed most of the day on the weekends!

PRONUNCIATION: Final -s/-es sound

5 ▶1.1 Listen to the verb endings in these sentences. Check (✓) the correct column.

	/s/	/z/	/əz/
1 He <u>wants</u> to be a doctor.			
2 Silvia <u>goes</u> to college.			
3 Betty <u>likes</u> chocolate.			
4 Susie <u>watches</u> TV in the evenings.			
5 Paul <u>changes</u> clothes twice a day.			
6 Adam <u>knows</u> my brother.			
7 Lily <u>thinks</u> soccer is boring.			
8 Mr. Jones <u>teaches</u> us French.			

2

SKILLS 1B

LISTENING: Listening for the main idea

1 ▶ 1.2 Listen to Daniel and Laura's conversation. Are the sentences about Daniel true (T) or false (F)?

1 He wants to stop using his cell phone for a few weeks. _____
2 He wants to use his free time differently. _____
3 He wants to spend less time with other people. _____
4 He goes to the movies a lot. _____
5 He wants to go out more. _____
6 He doesn't want to spend any time in the kitchen. _____

2 ▶ 1.2 Complete the sentences with the correct contractions. Then listen again and check.

1 So, Daniel, I hear you _____ going to use your phone this month.
2 At least, when _____ not at work.
3 I realized that I _____ actually do anything these days.
4 We never go out together these days. I mean, _____ crazy.
5 I _____ live my life like this!
6 I watch movies at home on my laptop instead. It _____ good.
7 Oh, and my _____ staying with me for a while.
8 _____ really good at baking.

3 Complete the sentences with the verbs in the box. There are two extra verbs.

| stay | collect | play | go on | shop | bake |
| get | go out | spend | get together with | | |

1 He wants to _____ more time with his family.
2 She goes running three times a week to _____ in shape.
3 Do you often _____ your friends after work?
4 Some of the kids _____ chess at lunchtime.
5 In our free time we like to _____ cakes.
6 Do your parents _____ much exercise?
7 I don't _____ social media much.
8 They don't go to the shopping center. They prefer to _____ online.

3

1C LANGUAGE

GRAMMAR: Present continuous and simple present

1 Choose the correct options to complete the sentences.

1 Kathy can't go out today. ____ her essay.
   a She's finishing   b She finishes

2 This soup is very salty. ____ it.
   a I'm not liking   b I don't like

3 ____ a lot in your country?
   a Is it snowing   b Does it snow

4 ____ for exams right now.
   a We're studying   b We study

5 Is that Emir? ____ his brother.
   a I'm knowing   b I know

6 Sophia is busy. ____ dinner.
   a She's cooking   b She cooks

7 Luis works as a journalist. ____ articles about sports.
   a He's writing   b He writes

8 I can go with you. ____ anything right now.
   a I'm not doing   b I don't do

9 ____ his daughter to school every morning.
   a Sam is taking   b Sam takes

10 ____ to the gym with you very often?
   a Is Raul going   b Does Raul go

2 Complete the sentences with the simple present or present continuous form of the verbs in the box.

> think   not play   walk   do   be
> work   wear   have

1 Mr. Silva _____ past our house every morning.

2 Mom and Dad _____ their lunch right now.

3 Laura _____ in a café for three months this summer.

4 Luca _____ soccer very often.

5 Olga and Sergei _____ from Russia.

6 _____ Helen usually _____ her homework in the evenings?

7 Maria _____ our new teacher is great.

8 Jorge _____ a jacket today.

VOCABULARY: Useful verbs

3 Choose the correct verbs to complete the sentences.

1 I often ____ my keys. It's very annoying!   miss   lose
2 Pablo usually ____ our swimming races.   wins   earns
3 Susie ____ really happy, doesn't she?   looks like   looks
4 I'm cold! Let's ____ home.   go back   come back
5 Emma's ____ a blue coat today.   wearing   carrying
6 Can you ____ me to call Alan later?   remember   remind
7 I'm ____ for Francesca to arrive.   hoping   waiting
8 Are you ____ your vacation?   looking   expecting
                                                     forward to
9 Emma often ____ me about her friends.   says   tells
10 I need to ____ some documents to Mr.   take   bring
   Smith's office.

4 Complete the conversation with verbs from exercise 3 in the correct tense.

Anna Are you going to Jorge and Sara's wedding? I'm really ¹_____ it.

Laura Yes, I am! But I can only buy them a small present, because I'm not ²_____ very much money at the moment.

Anna Never mind! Do you have anything to wear to the wedding?

Laura No, but my sister ³_____ from her vacation tomorrow, and she has so many amazing dresses.

Anna I ⁴_____ she'll have something perfect!

Laura Yes, definitely. Every week she ⁵_____ home something new from the shopping center!

Anna By the way, do you ⁶_____ Carlos, Jorge's best friend?

Laura Yes, I do. He's the tall guy who ⁷_____ Zac Efron, isn't he? He's great—I really ⁸_____ he'll be at the wedding.

Anna Of course he will. Jorge ⁹_____ he's like a brother to him. He works in France in the winter, and Jorge really ¹⁰_____ him when he's gone.

PRONUNCIATION: -ng sound

5 ▶1.3 Practice saying the sentences. Listen, check, and repeat.

1 I'm bringing Julio to the meeting.
2 He's studying French in college.
3 She's carrying a young child.
4 Are they running in the park?
5 They're singing my favorite song.
6 I'm taking a strong box for the heavy books.
7 She's wearing a long dress.

4

SKILLS 1D

WRITING: Making notes

1 Read Cristina's blog about three important people in her life. Number the information for each person in the order it appears.

Bianca:
a personality ___
b relationship to Cristina ___
c age ___

Clara Fuentes:
a how she helped Cristina ___
b her job ___
c relationship to Cristina ___

Grandpa:
a personality ___
b relationship to Cristina's father ___
c lifestyle ___

Lots of people say that their brothers and sisters are annoying, but I love being with my sister, Bianca. That's probably ¹_____ I don't live with her all the time! I'm away at college, but she's only six, ²_____ our relationship is kind of different from most sisters. Bianca's really funny, and she makes me laugh a lot. When we go out, people sometimes think I'm her mom. I hope I have a daughter like her one day—but not yet!

The second person who is very important to me is my neighbor, Clara Fuentes. She has an unusual job for a woman ³_____ she's an airline pilot. Clara told me once that women can do any job in the world! ⁴_____ I'm studying engineering. There are only three women in my class, but I love it and I'm good at it.

Person number three is my grandpa, who is my dad's father. My dad has five brothers. ⁵_____ our family is so big! Grandpa lives alone, but we all visit him, ⁶_____ he's never lonely! He is interested in all of us, and always wants to know about our lives. He's very kind and generous and everyone loves him.

2 Complete 1–6 in the blog with *because*, *so*, or *That's why*, and decide if each one is a reason or result.

3 Think of three important people in your life. Write notes about them.

Person 1	
name	
relationship to me	
his/her life: job, where he/she lives, etc.	
his/her personality	
why he/she is important to me	

Person 2	
name	
relationship to me	
his/her life: job, where he/she lives, etc.	
his/her personality	
why he/she is important to me	

Person 3	
name	
relationship to me	
his/her life: job, where he/she lives, etc.	
his/her personality	
why he/she is important to me	

4 Write a blog about three important people in your life.
- Use some or all of your notes from exercise 3.
- Write as many ideas as you can about the main topics.
- Choose the best ideas and organize them into paragraphs.
- Include at least three sentences with *because*, *so*, or *That's why*.

1 REVIEW and PRACTICE

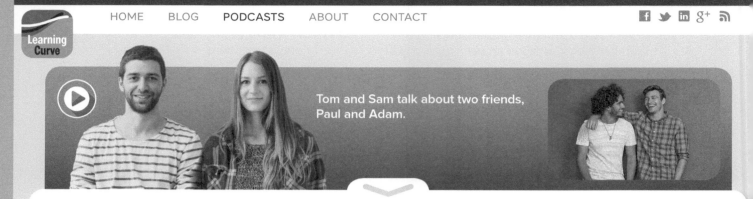

LISTENING

1 ▶ 1.4 Listen to the podcast. Check (✓) the things Paul talks about.

a Adam's hobbies _____
b how he met Adam _____
c Adam's personality _____
d what he has in common with Adam _____
e Adam's children _____
f where Paul lives _____

2 ▶ 1.4 Listen again. Choose the correct options to complete the sentences.

1 Paul sees Adam
   a most evenings.
   b when they go running.
   c at work.
2 Paul says that Adam
   a enjoys going out.
   b has a lot of friends.
   c isn't very sociable.
3 Adam spends some of his free time
   a playing games with his sons.
   b playing sports with his sons.
   c teaching his sons Spanish.
4 Paul and Adam
   a always go to concerts with each other.
   b belong to the same gym.
   c like different types of music.
5 Paul says that Adam
   a never talks about his friends.
   b has the same job as Paul.
   c helps Paul with his problems.
6 Adam
   a is always very serious.
   b makes Paul laugh.
   c can sometimes be selfish.

READING

1 Read the blog about friendship. Check (✓) the correct sentence.

a Teresa and Livia are about the same age. _____
b Teresa and Livia have different jobs. _____
c Teresa and Livia both have children. _____
d Teresa isn't married. _____
e Livia is Teresa's only friend. _____

2 Are the sentences true (T), false (F), or isn't there enough information to decide (N)?

1 According to the writer, nobody can be friends with someone who is 25 years older. _____
2 Teresa and Livia work in the same place. _____
3 They often spend time together. _____
4 Teresa thinks that Livia gets tired more often than Teresa. _____
5 Teresa has a lot of problems with her children. _____
6 Teresa discusses all her problems with her mother, too. _____
7 Teresa and Livia always like the same books. _____
8 Teresa learns more from Livia than Livia learns from Teresa. _____
9 Livia always likes the clothes that Teresa suggests for her. _____
10 Livia enjoys going out with Teresa. _____

REVIEW and PRACTICE 1

HOME BLOG PODCASTS ABOUT CONTACT

Sam writes about friendship.

What're 25 years between friends?

What do you think of when you hear or use the phrase "best friend"? Probably two people of about the same age. When we think of relationships between older and younger people, we may have negative feelings about them. How often do we hear older people complaining that the young are lazy, selfish, and rude? Or young people saying that older people don't understand them? But does it have to be like that? Teresa Fuentes, 28, and Livia Robles, 53, say it doesn't!

Teresa

Livia and I work together in a large school. She works in the school office, and I'm a history teacher. We usually have lunch together, and sometimes we go out in the evenings, too. Livia may be 25 years older than me, but she's so much fun, and sometimes I think she has more energy than me! That's probably because I'm taking care of three small children, and her children are grown up.

I love having an older friend because Livia is always patient and she has a lot of life experience. She's interested in my life and gives me lots of good advice, especially about the kids. She's not afraid to be honest if she thinks I'm doing something wrong. I often talk to her about things I can't discuss with my mom because I don't want to worry her. But to me, Livia isn't like another mother—she's just Livia, my friend!

Livia

I think it's a really good thing to have friends of all ages. Talking to people with different lives and different experiences makes you think about things in a new way. Teresa and I often discuss the books we're reading, and it's interesting how different our opinions can be!

Teresa says she learns from me, but I learn a lot from her, too—about things like cooking and gardening. She and her husband grow all their own vegetables! She loves fashion too, and often suggests things for me that I wouldn't choose myself: This pink jacket I'm wearing now, for example.

And having a friend in her twenties means that I can go out and have fun. She even sometimes takes me to nightclubs! Being with Teresa and her friends reminds me of being young and, anyway, there's a lot more to life than housework and watching TV!

UNIT 2

Stories and pictures

2A — LANGUAGE

GRAMMAR: Simple past and time expressions

1 Order the letters to make the simple past form of the verbs.

1. Anna usually rides her bike to work, but today she **kedlaw** _____.
2. Daniel **okot** _____ a bus to college yesterday.
3. Last night Marta **newt** _____ to a concert.
4. Did you **grinb** _____ any money with you?
5. We **ederbmerem** _____ to send Tim a birthday card.
6. I **rited** _____ to open the door, but it was locked.
7. Beatriz **retow** _____ him a letter to explain the problem.
8. I **dretsta** _____ my new job in January.
9. We **beldimc** _____ to the top of the mountain.
10. Sara **tens** _____ me an e-mail with the details.

2 Complete Rafael's postcard with the simple past of the verbs in parentheses.

Hi Mom and Dad!
We ¹_____ (get) here safely yesterday. The trip ²_____ (be) fine. Daniel's dad ³_____ (meet) us at the airport and ⁴_____ (drive) us to their house. In the evening we ⁵_____ (go) to the movies. On the way, we ⁶_____ (stop) at a café and ⁷_____ (have) some pizza. We ⁸_____ (get) home after midnight—I'm very tired today!
Love from Rafael

VOCABULARY: -ed/-ing adjectives

3 Complete 1–6 with an adjective from each pair in the box.

amazed / amazing   annoyed / annoying   excited / exciting
confused / confusing   interested / interesting   tired / tiring

1. I'm _____ by these instructions. They're not very clear.
2. My neighbors are _____. They're so noisy.
3. Eric's brother is very _____ in cars.
4. She's very _____ about her vacation. She's really looking forward to it.
5. Ted felt _____ after running ten kilometers.
6. We went to a fantastic restaurant last night. The food was _____!

4 Complete the sentences with -ed or -ing adjectives.

1. I often fall asleep in my math classes. They're really b_____!
2. Betty was di_____ when she failed her driving test.
3. I'm su_____ to see Manuel. He doesn't usually come here.
4. Cristina's really te_____ of snakes, but her sister's not scared of them.
5. It's so em_____ when you can't remember someone's name!
6. We love spending the day at the beach. It's very re_____.

PRONUNCIATION: -ed endings

5 ▶ 2.1 Listen and (circle) the sound that you hear at the end of the underlined verb. Listen, check, and repeat.

1	We <u>climbed</u> to the top of the mountain.	/t/	/əd/	/d/
2	I <u>decided</u> to go to Michael's house.	/t/	/əd/	/d/
3	Eduardo <u>looked</u> at the photograph.	/t/	/əd/	/d/
4	The cook <u>experimented</u> with new dishes.	/t/	/əd/	/d/
5	I <u>traveled</u> to Rome by train.	/t/	/əd/	/d/
6	In the evening, we <u>watched</u> TV.	/t/	/əd/	/d/
7	We <u>opened</u> our presents together.	/t/	/əd/	/d/
8	She <u>worked</u> all day yesterday.	/t/	/əd/	/d/

SKILLS 2B

READING: Approaching a text

1 Read the title and the first three lines of the text. What do you think it is about?
  a A man who doesn't say much.
  b A man who isn't as quiet as people think.
  c A man who shouts a lot.

2 Look at the photograph. Who do you think the people are?

3 Match topics 1–4 with paragraph headings A–D.
  1 A shy person doing something brave. _____
  2 A couple getting married. _____
  3 Something that is written down. _____
  4 People wondering what someone will do. _____

Robin Jones thought her grandfather was a quiet, shy man. Then she read her grandmother's diary and learned about the one time he wasn't …

A All in black and white
Grandma's diary was about the year 1950. Every day she wrote about her life. Before June, it was mostly about her job at a jewelry store and the lives of the other young women who worked there. But after June, she started to mention a regular customer—a nice young man who came in to buy a necklace for his mother. Then he came back the next day, and the next, and the next …

B Will he, won't he?
Each time, he asked Grandma to help him, but he never bought anything else. Eventually, one of the other salespeople said to Grandma, "I know why he comes. It's to see you!" They all expected Grandpa to ask her out, but he never did.

C The mouse becomes a lion
Then one day everything changed. Grandpa was in the store when a man ran in with a gun. He pointed it at Grandma and told her to give him a diamond ring. In an instant, that shy young man changed. "Drop the gun!" he shouted, and pushed the man to the floor. "Don't you dare frighten that young woman! She's going to be my wife one day!"

The quiet man?

D Wedding bells
After that, the police came and arrested the robber, and everyone said that Grandpa was a hero. But there was something Grandma still wasn't sure about. "Did you just ask me to marry you?" she asked Grandpa. Grandpa just smiled, but two months later they got married!

4 Are the sentences true (T) or false (F)?
  1 Grandma wrote about Grandpa before June. _____
  2 Grandpa bought lots of jewelry from the store. _____
  3 The other salespeople thought Grandpa liked Grandma. _____
  4 The robber tried to steal a necklace from the store. _____
  5 Grandpa was very angry with the robber. _____
  6 The police took the robber away. _____
  7 The people in the store thought Grandpa was brave. _____
  8 Grandma always knew that Grandpa wanted to marry her. _____

5 Complete the sentences about the text with *then*, *after*, or *later*.
  1 _____ Robin Jones read her grandmother's diary, she had a different idea about her grandfather.
  2 One day, Grandpa came to the store to buy a necklace. A day _____, he came into the store again.
  3 _____ that, Grandma started to write about him in her diary.
  4 _____ a while, the other salespeople realized that Grandpa was coming to see Grandma.
  5 A man pointed a gun at Grandma. _____ he tried to steal a ring.
  6 A few minutes _____, the police arrived.

9

2C — LANGUAGE

GRAMMAR: Question forms

1 Order the words to make questions.

1 did / do / what / on vacation / they

_____?

2 need / we / to buy / do / a ticket

_____?

3 did / the movies / who / with / go to / Bruno

_____?

4 is / apartment / where / new / Sally's

_____?

5 do / how / to / the station / get / you

_____?

6 do / dinner / you / want / what / for

_____?

7 the milk / in / is / the refrigerator

_____?

8 play / does / sister / the violin / your

_____?

2 Complete the questions to match the answers. Write one or two words in each space.

1 _____ are you _____?
I'm from Peru.

2 _____ is your English teacher?
Mrs. Smith is my English teacher.

3 _____ you _____ Max today?
No, I didn't see Max today.

4 _____ you move to New York?
I moved to New York in 2015.

5 _____ his name?
His name is Louis.

6 _____ Maria a teacher?
Yes, she is.

7 _____ Larry very angry?
No, Larry wasn't very angry.

8 _____ you travel to Lima?
We traveled to Lima by plane.

VOCABULARY: Life stages

3 Read about Kazuo's life. Order the phrases. Write 1–6.

a engaged to Eriko _____

b children (two boys) _____

c retired 1990 _____

d born Kyoto, 1930 _____

e married Eriko _____

f elementary and middle school, Tokyo _____

4 Complete the text about Kazuo's life. Write one word in each space.

KAZUO

Kazuo [1]_____ born in Kyoto, in Japan, in 1930. His family moved when he was still a baby and he grew [2]_____ in Tokyo, where he [3]_____ to elementary and middle school. After Kazuo [4]_____ high school, he [5]_____ to college to study medicine. At the university, he met a girl named Eriko. They [6]_____ engaged, but they waited until graduating from college before they [7]_____ married. They [8]_____ two children. Kazuo worked as a doctor for 30 years. In 1990, after a successful career, he [9]_____ and spent the next twenty years doing what he loved: painting. Sadly, Kazuo [10]_____ in 2015, at the age of 85.

PRONUNCIATION: Question intonation

5 ▶2.2 Listen to the questions. Does the intonation go up (U) or down (D) at the end?

1 How do you spell your name? _____

2 Do you like cheese? _____

3 Is their house very big? _____

4 When is her birthday? _____

5 Where do you live? _____

6 Did you see Peter? _____

7 Was Anna very angry? _____

8 Who did you go on vacation with? _____

SKILLS 2D

SPEAKING: Telling a personal story

1 ▶ 2.3 Listen to Emma tell Dominic a personal story. Check (✓) the phrases you hear.

a What happened? _____
b Did I ever tell you about the time …? _____
c That's amazing! _____
d Really? _____
e What did you do then? _____
f Oh no! _____
g You're joking! _____
h That's awful! _____
i That reminds me of … _____
j Lucky you! _____
k You poor thing! _____
l You'll never guess … _____
m I felt really … _____

2 ▶ 2.3 Listen again. Which of the phrases in exercise 1 do Emma and Dominic use to do these things?

1 Emma tells Dominic something surprising. _____
2 Dominic shows sympathy. _____ _____ _____
3 Emma describes her emotions after the accident happened. _____
4 Dominic shows that he is interested. _____
5 Dominic says that something similar happened to him. _____

3 ▶ 2.4 Listen to six people talking. Choose the best way of showing interest and say it aloud.

1 *You poor thing! / What did he do then? / That's amazing!*
2 *What happened? / Oh no! / Lucky you!*
3 *Great! / That's awful! / You're joking!*
4 *What did he do then? / You poor thing! / Great!*
5 *What happened? / Lucky you! / Oh no!*
6 *That's amazing! / That's awful! / What happened?*

4 ▶ 2.5 Listen and check your answers to exercise 3.

5 ▶ 2.6 Match the sentence parts. Say them aloud. Then listen and check.

1 Something similar _____   a nervous about meeting her.
2 That reminds _____   b tell you about my flight to Tokyo.
3 You'll never guess _____ c you about the time I met Zac Efron?
4 Let me _____   d so amazing to discover we have the same name!
5 Can you _____   e imagine how scared I was?
6 I felt _____   f happened to me when I was a student.
7 Did I ever tell _____   g what happened to Regina yesterday.
8 It was _____   h me of the time I lost my passport.

11

2 REVIEW and PRACTICE

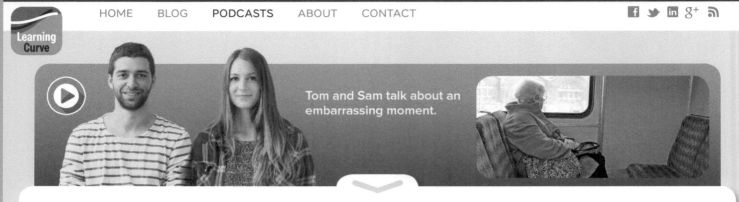

LISTENING

1 ▶ 2.7 Listen to the podcast. Choose the best summary.

a Maria made friends with an old lady.
b Maria dropped someone's bag on the train.
c Maria upset a complete stranger.

2 ▶ 2.7 Listen again. Choose the correct options to complete the sentences.

1 Maria was surprised by
   a how old the lady was.
   b how nice the lady looked.
   c how interesting the lady was.
2 Maria and the lady had
   a nothing to talk about.
   b little to talk about.
   c a lot to talk about.
3 When she stood up, the lady appeared
   a shorter.
   b younger.
   c older.
4 Maria tried to help the lady by
   a supporting her with her arm.
   b supporting her with her arm and holding her bag.
   c holding her bag.
5 Maria dropped the lady's
   a candy.
   b bag.
   c stick.
6 The bag fell on
   a the track.
   b the platform.
   c a man.
7 The old lady was
   a very angry.
   b pretty calm.
   c too upset to talk.
8 The man helped them by
   a mending the bag.
   b picking up the medicine bottle.
   c getting the bag back.

READING

1 Read the blog about games that use pictures. Complete 1–6 with the adjectives in the box.

annoyed   disappointing   confusing
surprised   interesting   boring

2 Are the sentences true (T), false (F), or isn't there enough information to decide (N)?

1 The writer's family plays games together every Christmas. ____
2 The writer's sister got more correct answers than their father. ____
3 The writer's mother couldn't name any of the famous people. ____
4 The Spot the Ball competition started in the 1970s. ____
5 The writer's mother played Spot the Ball more than once. ____
6 The writer's father was angry when his wife won a prize. ____
7 The writer's parents didn't earn much money. ____
8 Spot the Ball is less popular today than in the past. ____
9 Spot the Ball is a more difficult competition today than in the 1970s. ____
10 The writer prefers games that use pictures of animals. ____

REVIEW and PRACTICE 2

HOME **BLOG** PODCASTS ABOUT CONTACT

Tom writes about his favorite games.

Games that use pictures

I'm an amateur photographer, so it's probably not surprising that I love games that are based on images. Last Christmas I organized a quiz for my family. I selected images of different people in the news that year and everyone earned a point for each person they could name correctly. My sister thought it was [1]_____, so she didn't really try. I was really [2]_____ when my dad won. He even managed to recognize Taylor Swift!

Then my parents told me about a game named "Spot the Ball" that was very popular in the 1970s. It was a simple game found in lots of newspapers. You looked at an action shot of a soccer game, but the ball was removed from the photo, and you had to say where you thought it should be. Apparently, my dad found it really [3]_____ and played it every week. But Mom got very [4]_____ with him because he wanted to discuss exactly where all the players were looking. Mom used to guess, and one week she won! She only won $100, but that was a lot of money in those days.

Later, I read an article about the game, and I was amazed that the last time anyone won the jackpot prize, was in 2004! About three million people used to play it every week in the 1970s, but now there are only about 14,000 players. I think that's a little [5]_____ because it's a lot of fun.

There's another game that I really enjoy that uses images. You see a very small part of something in detail, and you have to figure out what it is. There are entire blogs with these kinds of pictures; one of my favorites is *http://floorsix.blogspot.co.uk/*. Some of the images are really [6]_____, but to me, that's what makes them even more interesting. I love asking myself questions about them: What does it look like? Is it an animal? Is that part of a machine? How big is it really? Do you want to take a guess? Look at these three images and try to figure out what they are.

UNIT 3 Keep on traveling

3A LANGUAGE

GRAMMAR: Comparatives, superlatives, (not) as ... as

1 Choose the correct options to complete the sentences.

1 The weather here is hotter _____ it is in Germany.
   a most   b than   c as

2 My sister isn't _____ tall as me.
   a as   b than   c more

3 This sofa is _____ comfortable than the other one.
   a most   b as   c more

4 Matias is the _____ boy in our class!
   a funniest   b more funny   c funnier

5 For me, science is _____ class of all!
   a the most bad b worst   c the worst

6 Is your house _____ Rafael's?
   a as big than   b as big as   c more big than

7 Stella makes _____ best cakes in the world!
   a most   b the   c as

8 This is the _____ expensive restaurant in the city.
   a most   b as   c more

2 Complete the conversation with comparative and superlative forms of the adjectives in the box.

> far   cheap   early   important   lazy
> close   crowded   interesting

A Hi, Daniel. I heard you moved to a new apartment.

B Yes, I moved downtown because I wanted to be ¹_____ to work. Taking public transportation was so expensive. I can walk everywhere now, which is a lot ²_____.

A I know! I live even ³_____ away than you did. It costs so much, and I think it's the ⁴_____ train in the country; it's always completely full in the mornings.

B Maybe you should move, as well! I find living downtown a lot ⁵_____ than living in the suburbs. There's so much to do here.

A I could never live downtown. My pets are the ⁶_____ things in my life. I couldn't live without them!

B Maybe you should try taking an ⁷_____ train?

A Probably, but I hate getting up in the morning. I'm the ⁸_____ member of my family!

VOCABULARY: Useful adjectives

3 Order the letters to make adjectives.

1 I didn't sleep well because the hotel bed was so FRONTBAUMCELO. _____

2 I need to pack my suitcase again because it's too SYSEM. _____

3 I didn't think the beach would be so TIQUE on the weekend. _____

4 Athens is NICETAN. People have lived there for over 7,000 years. _____

5 The Eiffel Tower is the most SOMAFU building in Paris. _____

6 His store sells LUNUSUA souvenirs that you won't find anywhere else. _____

4 Complete the text about Tokyo. The first letters are given.

> With nearly 40 million people living there, Tokyo is one of the most ¹ c __ __ __ __ __ __ cities in the world. And it has more cars than anywhere else in Japan, almost 70 million of them, so it's extremely ² p __ __ __ __ __ __ __ , as well. But Tokyo is also one of the most popular places for foreign tourists to visit. It's very safe and, although it's extremely ³ b __ __ __ , many people love the fact that it's really ⁴ l __ __ __ __ __ __ and that there's plenty to see and do. Some visitors may think that ⁵ m __ __ __ __ __ __ buildings like the Sugamo-Shinkin bank, built in 2011, are ⁶ u __ __ __ , but others think they are beautiful and love the fact that they use some of the best 21st century technology.

PRONUNCIATION: Sentence stress

5 ▶3.1 Circle the underlined word that is most stressed. Listen, check, and repeat.

1 Albert is the best student in his class.

2 My soup doesn't taste as good as Jasmine's.

3 Tokyo is closer to Mumbai than to São Paulo.

4 Is Lady Gaga more famous than Taylor Swift?

5 My car is the most expensive thing I own.

6 Sophia's essay was a lot better than Helena's.

7 It's quieter in the country than in the city.

8 I'm feeling a little happier than I was before.

SKILLS 3B

LISTENING: Identifying key points

1 ▶ 3.2 Listen to Joe and Sara talking about vacations. Are the sentences true (T) or false (F)?

1 Sara visits a lot of cities. _____
2 Joe and Sara don't enjoy the same types of vacations. _____
3 Sara doesn't like traveling alone. _____

2 ▶ 3.2 Listen again and choose the correct words to complete the sentences.

1 Sara really likes *cities / beaches / hotels*.
2 Joe doesn't enjoy *going to the beach / going hiking / going abroad*.
3 Sara doesn't like *museums / sunbathing / churches*.
4 A week before Sara leaves, she *makes hotel reservations / packs her suitcase / books a flight*.
5 The night before Sara leaves, she *plans her sightseeing / eats out / packs a suitcase*.
6 Sara spends most of her vacation *by herself / with other people / on guided tours*.
7 Sara likes traveling alone because she can *choose what to do / read more / go sightseeing*.
8 Sara takes a book when she *goes sightseeing / eats out by herself / goes on guided tours*.

3 ▶ 3.3 <u>Underline</u> the key words that are most likely to be stressed by the speaker in these sentences. Listen and check.

1 The museums are crowded in the summer.
2 Did you book a flight?
3 We could rent a car at the airport.
4 I'd love to travel abroad.
5 The barbecue at the hotel was fantastic.
6 They stay in a beautiful house by the ocean.

4 Complete the sentences with the correct form of the verbs in the box.

| reserve buy eat out go |
| have rent visit stay |

1 We both love to _____ at the local restaurants.
2 Could you _____ a double room for my parents, please?
3 Let's _____ a car to drive around the island.
4 My little sister likes to _____ a few souvenirs to take home.
5 My aunt and uncle usually _____ camping in the summer.
6 Lucy and James are _____ at a beach resort.
7 Today we _____ the local attractions.
8 Peter always _____ a great time when he's on vacation.

15

3C LANGUAGE

GRAMMAR: Past continuous and simple past

1 Order the words to make sentences. Add commas where necessary.

1 Alba was / café when / waiting / I arrived / in the
   _____
2 working when / Nancy / was / I / her / left
   _____
3 taking / called / Sara / when Lara / a shower / was
   _____
4 he was / Ed lived / at home while / studying / law
   _____
5 I looked / was smiling / that he / at Dad / and saw
   _____
6 still waiting / were / to get in / when the show / started / we
   _____
7 her homework / book while / Marian was / I read a / finishing
   _____
8 into the / we were / house while / the thieves / got / sleeping
   _____
9 watching TV / cooking while / were / Mom was / the kids
   _____
10 shopping her friend / while Paola was / went to / the museum
   _____

2 Complete each sentence with the verbs in parentheses. Write one past continuous and one simple past form.

1 When we _____ Carlos, he _____ his car. (see, clean)
2 Marta _____ for the bus when she _____. (run, fall)
3 Anna _____ Julia while she _____ to class. (meet, walk)
4 Hugo _____ his leg when he _____ tennis. (hurt, play)
5 My phone _____ while I _____. (ring, drive)
6 When Rick _____ his hair, he _____ shampoo in his eyes. (wash, get)
7 Emma _____ late for class because she _____ to Luisa. (be, talk)
8 The plane _____ above the ocean when the storm _____. (fly, start)
9 My sister _____ my phone when I _____. (take, not look)
10 When Jackie _____ her shopping, someone _____ her bag. (do, steal)

PRONUNCIATION: was/were

3 ▶ 3.4 Practice saying the sentences. Pay attention to the pronunciation of was /wəz/ and were /wər/. Listen, check, and repeat.

1 What were you doing at five o'clock yesterday?
2 I was expecting Monica to call.
3 Rafael was talking to his friend.
4 We were playing outside, but it started to rain.
5 Adam was watching TV while I worked.
6 While you were sleeping, I baked a cake.
7 I was doing my homework all morning.
8 Clara was running when the accident happened.

SKILLS 3D

WRITING: Writing a narrative

1 Read two paragraphs from different parts of a story about a vacation incident. Choose the correct verbs.

A They went up to the check-in desk, where a woman ¹*checked / was checking* everyone's tickets and passports. Simon ²*gave / was giving* her their passports. The woman took them, then looked at Simon strangely. "Why did you give me this?" she asked. Then Simon and Gabrielle ³*got / were getting* a terrible shock. They didn't have Gabrielle's passport. They had Simon's passport and Simon's old passport!

B Simon and Gabrielle sat in the car. They felt happy and were talking to Simon's brother, Toby, who ⁴*drove / was driving* them to the airport for their skiing trip. They had to be there by 5:30 a.m., and there weren't any buses that early. They were tired, but excited. They had a good trip and Toby ⁵*left / was leaving* them outside the airport. They thanked him and ⁶*went / were going* to get their flight.

2 Read two more paragraphs from different parts of the story. Choose the correct adjectives or adverbs.

C However, when she got back, the airline staff was very ¹*helpful / helpfully*. They ²*kind / kindly* found her a seat on a later flight and she didn't have to pay extra. When she arrived in Denver, the shuttle to the ski resort had already left, but it was easy to get a bus there. She arrived in time for a ³*delicious / deliciously* dinner, and she quickly forgave Simon. After all, anyone can make a mistake and everything worked out in the end!

D The woman told them ⁴*rude / rudely* that Gabrielle couldn't travel. She said that Simon should get on the plane. "But he's the one who made the mistake!" said Gabrielle. She was really angry. However, there was nothing they could do. Gabrielle had to rent a car and drive back home for her passport. It was a fast trip, but she still missed the flight. She felt very worried and ⁵*miserable / miserably*.

3 Look at these sentences from the text. Rewrite them using adverbs instead of adjectives.

1 They felt happy and were talking.
   They talked _____.
2 They had a good trip.
   The trip went _____.
3 "But he's the one who made the mistake!" said Gabrielle. She was really angry.
   "But he's the one who made the mistake!" said Gabrielle _____.
4 It was a fast trip, but she still missed the flight.
   She drove _____, but she still missed the flight.

4 Match 1–4 with paragraphs A–D.

1 The background (who, when, where) ____
2 A problem (what happened) ____
3 A resolution (how she solved the problem) ____
4 The ending (what happened in the end, how she felt) ____

5 Write a different last paragraph for the story.
- Use the ideas below or your own ideas.
- Write at least five sentences.
- Use the past continuous and the simple past correctly.
- Use adjectives and adverbs to make your paragraph more interesting.

> no plane until next day

> went to wrong ski resort

> Simon was waiting for her at the airport in Denver

> decided to stay home and not go skiing

> had a big argument with Simon

> had to pay for a new ticket

17

3 REVIEW and PRACTICE

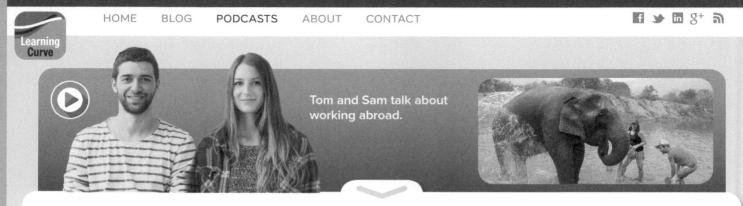

LISTENING

1 ▶ 3.5 Listen to the podcast. Circle True or False.

1 Mara worked with elephants in Thailand. — True / False
2 She found the work fairly easy. — True / False
3 The local people weren't very friendly. — True / False
4 Mara went to Thailand by herself. — True / False
5 One of the animals got sick. — True / False

2 ▶ 3.5 Listen again. Complete the sentences with a maximum of three words.

1 Mara says it was _____ to be so close to the animals.
2 Mara enjoyed being part of a _____.
3 The _____ made the work difficult for Mara.
4 Mara really enjoyed eating the _____.
5 Some of the people Mara worked with went to Thailand in _____.
6 Mara made _____ with people from around the world.
7 Mara says it's important to _____ a lot there because of the heat.
8 Mara felt better after someone gave her a large _____.

READING

1 Read the blog about four hotels. What do you think the word "quirkiest" in the heading means?

a most expensive
b most comfortable
c most unusual
d most famous

2 Match the descriptions to hotels A–D.

1 It is a very unusual shape. ____
2 It is difficult to get into. ____
3 It has no walls or roof. ____
4 It is made of a substance not normally used for buildings. ____

3 Choose the correct options to complete the sentences.

1 The Palacio de Sal is in an area
   a where salt is produced.
   b where many tourists want to go.
   c without normal building materials.
2 According to the blog, the restaurant at the Palacio de Sal
   a makes the best food in Bolivia.
   b makes food that is too salty.
   c makes a popular dish with salt.
3 Jules' Undersea Lodge is
   a in deep water.
   b only reached by taxi.
   c in shallow water.
4 People with heart problems can't stay at Jules' Undersea Lodge because
   a doctors can't reach the hotel.
   b it's not comfortable enough.
   c it is not safe for them.
5 In Dog Bark Park Inn, the beds are
   a in rooms in the dog.
   b shaped like dogs.
   c all in one big room.
6 At Dog Bark Park Inn, real dogs
   a have to be kept inside always.
   b are allowed to stay.
   c are not welcome.
7 According to the blog, it is good to stay in a treehouse because
   a you can stay outside all night.
   b you can see unusual animals.
   c it is cheaper than a hotel.
8 According to the blog, sleeping outside means you can experience
   a being with other people.
   b other aspects of nature.
   c waking up very early.

REVIEW and PRACTICE 3

HOME BLOG PODCASTS ABOUT CONTACT

Guest blogger Simon writes about hotels.

The world's best places to stay

Four of the world's quirkiest hotels

What do you want from a hotel? Something clean and comfortable for sure, but do you sometimes find your hotel room a little boring? Do you want your nights to be as much a part of your vacation adventure as your days? Here are four recommendations for a stay you'll never forget!

A Palacio de Sal

Most of us know about the ice hotels in countries like Sweden, where everything, even your bed, is made out of ice. But this hotel in Bolivia is even more unusual; it is made out of salt! About 350 km. south of the city of La Paz, this hotel is on the edge of the Salar de Uyuni, the world's largest salt plain. It was built using around a million blocks of salt. Visitors report that the food in the restaurant is excellent, especially their famous "salt chicken." There's even a swimming pool, filled with salt water, of course!

B Jules' Undersea Lodge

Usually you can get a taxi to your hotel, but not here! To stay in this hotel in Key Largo, you need to scuba dive to reach the entrance. Once you're there, you can watch fish through the windows of your room. Amazingly, there are hot showers, and you can even get pizza delivered! Because you have to dive to get to the lodge, you need to be in good shape. If you have heart problems, or are pregnant, this isn't the place for you!

C Dog Bark Park Inn

This has to be one of the strangest-looking hotels in the world. Owned by a husband and wife team in Idaho, U.S. the entire hotel looks like a large wooden dog! Four people can sleep inside the dog. There's even a room in its head. Rooms are filled with doggy decorations, and pets are, of course, welcome to stay with you!

D Chalkley's Treehouse

A safari is all about being outdoors, isn't it? It's all about the animals and the wide open spaces. So why go into a building or a tent at night when you could stay under the stars in this treehouse on the Lion Sands Game Reserve in South Africa? You can lie in bed and look up at the stars, watch the sun come up in the morning, and listen to the sound of animals and birds all around you. What could be more romantic?

19

The working world

GRAMMAR: *will*, *may*, and *might* for predictions

1 Read the statements. How likely is it that these things will happen? Write 1–8 in the correct columns.

1. Phelps will win the swimming competition.
2. She might lose the tennis match.
3. I don't think I will ever travel into space.
4. We might not finish the project on time.
5. They won't finish the work by Friday.
6. We may be able to go camping.
7. Of course, I may not get the job.
8. He'll get there before lunchtime.

Probably (More than 75%)	Possibly (50–75%)	Possibly not (25–50%)	Probably not (Less than 25%)
___	___	___	___
___	___	___	___

2 Complete the sentences with *will*, *won't*, *might*, *think*, or *don't think*.

1. I know for sure that Fatima _____ come to the party; she promised she would.
2. Gabriel _____ be home by six o'clock. It depends how much work he has to do.
3. I _____ Bernie will come to the movies. He's too busy.
4. He definitely _____ come with us on Tuesday. He only goes out on the weekends.
5. I _____ Victor will pass his exam. He's so smart and he's been studying hard.
6. We _____ go to the park for a picnic, although it depends on the weather.
7. I may visit Fernanda this evening, so I probably _____ go to the concert after all.
8. Don't worry, we _____ definitely get to the restaurant on time!
9. The sky looks fairly blue. I _____ that it'll rain today.
10. Our project is going very well, so we _____ it'll be a success.

VOCABULARY: Jobs

3 Order the letters to complete the names of the jobs.

1. sales S N R E P O _____
2. soccer O C C A H _____
3. fashion S E D G I N R E _____
4. movie R I D E C R O T _____
5. police F O F C I E R _____
6. tour U G I E D _____
7. security U D A R G _____
8. travel T E G A N _____

4 Complete the jobs. Some of the letters are given.

1. I asked an ac_____ for some advice about my money.
2. Luckily, the f_____s put out the fire very quickly.
3. We needed a l_____ to help us understand the contract.
4. Are all the fruit and vegetables at the market grown by local f_____?
5. She got her h_____ to cut her hair a lot shorter.
6. He's a well-known j_____ and writes for the national newspapers.
7. My cousin's a fashion m_____; she works for all the big designers.
8. We were given our room keys by the r_____ at the hotel.
9. Tomorrow I'll meet the s_____ who's going to operate on my knee.
10. Could you ask the w_____r to bring us some water with our meal?

PRONUNCIATION: *want/won't*

5 ▶ 4.1 Look at the underlined letters and listen to the sentences. Write 1 if the sound is /o/ and 2 if the sound is /a/. Listen, check, and repeat.

1. They use r<u>o</u>bots in the factory. ___
2. I really w<u>a</u>nt to see that movie. ___
3. I d<u>o</u>n't like cheese at all. ___
4. Do you kn<u>o</u>w where he lives? ___
5. My b<u>o</u>ss will be at the party tonight. ___
6. Isaac is looking for a j<u>o</u>b. ___
7. Manuel's mother used to be a m<u>o</u>del. ___
8. How <u>o</u>ld is your sister? ___

20

SKILLS 4B

READING: Skimming a text

1 Read topic sentences A–E in the article. Match each one with the most likely summary 1–5.

1 Evidence from a piece of research. _____
2 The value of time away from work. _____
3 How to reduce our use of handheld devices. _____
4 How technology affects our behavior. _____
5 Tips to help you concentrate. _____

A We're all multitaskers now, performing two or more tasks at the same time. Whether it's e-mailing a colleague while checking our smartphone, or writing an essay while catching up on the latest online celebrity gossip, we're all doing it. But should we? Well, recent research suggests it's time to stop demanding so much of our brain and go back to focusing on one thing at a time.

B Consider the results of a study of workers at a software company. When they stopped working on a major task to answer an e-mail or message, it took ten minutes to be able to fully concentrate again on the original task. Clearly this is not an efficient way of working. Training ourselves to concentrate isn't easy, but psychologist Maria Sylva has some tips:

C Let your mind focus on one thing at a time. Whatever task you're doing, make sure you give it your full attention. Giving 100% to the task in hand will help you work more quickly and more accurately. At the beginning, this might be tough, so start with short periods, say ten minutes, and gradually increase the amount of time.

D If your smartphone is the main source of distraction, leave it at home. If you really believe the next message you receive will be more interesting or important than your current activity, ask yourself why you are doing that activity.

E Give your brain a rest. You'll achieve more if, several times a day, you walk away from tasks that require concentration. And I mean "walk away." Don't just look away from your screen or stare out of the window. Get up and leave your desk. If possible, get some fresh air. Taking a complete break will help your brain to come up with new ideas.

2 Read the whole article, then choose the best ending for each sentence.

1 Maria Sylva wants us to consider whether
 a technology is a good thing in our lives.
 b we should be doing so many things at once.
 c we should use smartphones.
2 The study that she refers to shows that we lose time when we
 a change the task we are working on.
 b only use e-mail to communicate at work.
 c don't concentrate hard enough at work.
3 She claims we make fewer mistakes when we
 a work quickly.
 b work for ten minutes at a time.
 c concentrate fully on a task.
4 She tells us not to take a smartphone with us if
 a the messages we get on it are not interesting.
 b it prevents us from giving attention to what we are doing.
 c we leave the house.
5 She recommends
 a putting off tasks that need us to concentrate.
 b taking regular short breaks from work.
 c looking away from our screens occasionally.

3 Complete the text with the correct pronouns and possessive adjectives.

Maria Sylva is a life coach. ¹_____ advises people on how to manage ²_____ time. Most of ³_____ work is done inside companies where she coaches people at all levels, helping ⁴_____ perform to the best of their ability while ⁵_____ are working. Maria thoroughly enjoys her job and finds ⁶_____ very satisfying. Her aim is to help ⁷_____ accomplish the most that we possibly can during ⁸_____ working day.

21

4C LANGUAGE

GRAMMAR: *be going to* and present continuous

1 Choose the correct options to complete the sentences.

1 Pablo *going to study / is going to study / studying* medicine next year.
2 What *do you do / you doing / are you doing* this weekend?
3 I *going to / 'm going to / go to* finish my book tonight.
4 We're *visiting / visit / to visit* my parents next weekend.
5 I'm *meeting / meet / to meet* Daniel and Julia this evening if you'd like to join us.
6 We *going to / 're going to / 're going* buy our tickets tomorrow.
7 I *go to / 'm going to / going to* go running in half an hour.
8 My brother *is going to / is going to be / is being* at the festival.
9 Where *do you stay / are you staying / you stay* in Italy this summer?
10 I *go to / 'm going to / going to* ask Nancy if she wants to come to the theater.

2 Complete the sentences with the verbs in the box. Use the form in parentheses.

| paint | bake | speak | start | see | rent |

1 I can give Mary that book for you. I _____ her next week. (present continuous)
2 I think I _____ to Lily about the problem. (*be going to*)
3 I've decided I _____ a picture of my grandma's garden for her birthday. (*be going to*)
4 I'll be in Portugal for six months. I _____ an apartment in Lisbon. (present continuous)
5 I _____ a cake for Maria's birthday. (*be going to*)
6 Ismael _____ a new job in July. (present continuous)

VOCABULARY: Phrases about work

3 Match the two parts of the sentences.

1 I want to accept the job, but first we have to agree on ____   a her job.
2 She's so unhappy at work. I think she's going to quit ____   b an interview.
3 The interview went well, so I really hope I get ____   c form.
4 Think about the questions they might ask before you go for ____   d a salary.
5 The first step in applying for a job is to send in the application ____   e a résumé.
6 Henry is hoping that he's going to get a pay ____   f a job offer.
7 Larry is going to show me how to write ____   g work.
8 You must be looking forward to starting ____   h raise.

4 Complete the text about Lucas's job. The first letters are given.

Lucas started a ¹ c_____ in nursing five years ago. In January, he saw an ² a_____ for a job at the local hospital and decided to ³ a_____ for it. They invited him for an ⁴ i_____, which went very well. Two weeks later, they ⁵ o_____ him the job. Before he started work, he had to ⁶ t _____ a training course to improve his skills. Lucas is obviously great at his job. He has already received a ⁷ p_____, and he now has more responsibility and earns a big ⁸ s_____. In fact, he earns much more than I do!

PRONUNCIATION: *going to* and *want to*

5 ▶ 4.2 Listen to the sentences. Pay attention to the pronunciation of *going to* and *want to*. Listen again and repeat.

1 I'm going to apply for that position.
2 I want to quit this job.
3 I don't want to work in an office.
4 She's going to ask for a pay raise.
5 They're going to offer it to her.
6 He's going to write a résumé.

SKILLS 4D

SPEAKING: Telephone language

1 ▶ 4.3 Listen to a telephone conversation between Anne, who runs a company that offers disco lights and music for parties, and Ryan, a hotel receptionist. Number the phrases in the order you hear them.

a Could you ask him to call me back, please? ___
b Hello, … ___
c I'm afraid he's not available right now. ___
d How can I help you? ___
e Thanks for calling. ___
f Could I speak to …? ___
g Can I take a message? ___
h Can you tell him that …? ___

2 Complete the chart with options a–h from exercise 1.

Caller	Person being called
___	___
___	___
___	___
___	___

3 ▶ 4.4 Complete the conversation with phrases for dealing with difficulties. Then listen and check.

A Good morning, Hobson's department store. This is Helen. How can I help you?

B Hello, could I speak to someone in the electrical department, please?

A Sorry, could you ¹_____ a little louder? This line's really bad. And ²_____ speak more slowly, please?

B Yes, I'd like to speak to someone in the electrical department, please.

A Of course. I'll put you through to Simon Jones. He's in charge of electrical goods.
… Oh, I'm sorry. I'm afraid he's not available right now. He'll be back at eleven o'clock.

B Sorry, did ³_____ eleven?

A That's right. Should I ask him to call you?

B Yes, please. My number is 0755 511817.

A Could you ⁴_____, please?

B Yes, it's 0755 511817. Oh, and could you tell him that it needs to be as small as possible because I don't have much shelf space in my bedroom?

A I'm afraid I ⁵_____ that.

B Don't worry, I'll tell him when he calls.

A OK. And can I take your name, please?

B Robert Faux.

A Can ⁶_____ that, please?

B F-A-U-X.

A ⁷_____ A-U or E-U?

B A-U.

A Great, thank you. Simon will call you later. Goodbye.

23

4 REVIEW and PRACTICE

HOME BLOG **PODCASTS** ABOUT CONTACT

Tom and Sam talk about career changes.

LISTENING

1 ▶ 4.5 Listen to the podcast. Choose the correct statement.

a Larissa had problems at work and was extremely unhappy.
b Larissa didn't want to do the same thing forever.
c Larissa hated being an accountant and prefers being a teacher.

2 ▶ 4.5 Listen again. Are the sentences true (T) or false (F)?

1 Larissa earned a lot of money as an accountant. ____
2 The people she worked with were much younger than her. ____
3 She found an interesting job advertisement in a newspaper. ____
4 She was very surprised when she got the job. ____
5 She loved her time on the island. ____
6 She does not have definite plans for the future. ____
7 She might work as an accountant again. ____
8 She's definitely going to use her teaching skills in her next job. ____

READING

1 Read the blog about seven different careers. Match descriptions A–G with these jobs.

1 accountant   ____
2 fashion designer ____
3 hairdresser   ____
4 journalist   ____
5 lawyer   ____
6 receptionist   ____
7 salesperson   ____

2 Match each person with the job A–G that would be most suitable.

1 Evie is a patient and hardworking person. She enjoys talking to people and she always dresses well; her appearance is really important to her! ____

2 Jamie has a great imagination. He has always been good at art and is very good at math. He's not at all shy and is confident about learning new skills. ____

3 Hannah loves everything to do with fashion. She knows what makes people look great and what doesn't, and isn't afraid to tell them! She enjoys learning, too. ____

4 Marcus is very sociable; he's good at talking and gets along well with all kinds of people. He's also very honest and can usually tell if someone is lying. ____

5 Ray has excellent speaking and writing skills. He always did well in school and wants to study hard in college. He hates making mistakes! ____

24

REVIEW and PRACTICE 4

HOME BLOG PODCASTS ABOUT CONTACT

Guest blogger Marc writes about seven interesting careers.

Find the right career for you

A To be successful, you must be passionate about the truth. You'll need the confidence to ask people difficult questions. You may need to make yourself unpopular with important people. And, of course, you'll need to have excellent writing skills, as well as to be able to communicate clearly.

B This is a very creative job, so you need good drawing skills. However, you should be able to see your clothes in your head *before* you put your pencil to paper. But loving clothes and being good at art isn't enough. It's a competitive business and you need to understand your markets and be able to calculate the cost of materials, etc.

C This will only suit you if you're someone who pays attention to detail. Your work must be absolutely accurate. You also need good time-management skills: financial information is extremely important for a business and must be available at the right time. Many top people in this job are senior managers, so if you do well, you might be promoted quickly.

D You're often the first person a customer meets when they visit a company or a hotel, so you must look smart and communicate in a friendly, professional way. You might have to deal with difficult or rude people, so you need to be calm and polite. You don't need a lot of qualifications, but you will need to use your firm's computer and phone systems.

E If you think you'll be good at this, don't do it! You need to be *great*, not good! The best people are extremely confident and excellent communicators, but that doesn't mean talking all the time. You need to listen, too. Above all, you need to know when it's worth pushing, and when to walk away.

F For such a competitive career, you'll need excellent grades to be able to get a degree. You'll need to analyze information quickly and accurately. And using language effectively is essential for understanding technical documents and communicating with clients. You must be able to express yourself clearly and logically.

G This is a creative job—up to a point! Relationships are important, too, and you can earn respect by giving clients good advice. There's no point giving a perfect cut if it doesn't suit someone's face and features. You don't have to do particularly well in school, but you need great technical skills. The best professionals continue to take courses throughout their career.

UNIT 5

Mind and body

5A LANGUAGE

GRAMMAR: should/shouldn't

1 Match problems 1–8 with the best advice and circle *should* or *shouldn't* in a–h.

1 My car keeps breaking down. ____
2 I feel so tired all the time. ____
3 I'm extremely stressed at work. ____
4 I never have enough money to go on vacation. ____
5 I have a lot of problems with my teeth. ____
6 I'm bored with going to the same restaurant. ____
7 I sometimes feel very lonely. ____
8 I never get good grades on my homework. ____

a You *should / shouldn't* spend so much on clothes.
b You *should / shouldn't* ask your teacher's advice.
c You *should / shouldn't* stay up late.
d You *should / shouldn't* try the one that just opened.
e You *should / shouldn't* make some new friends.
f You *should / shouldn't* buy a better one.
g You *should / shouldn't* eat candy every day.
h You *should / shouldn't* speak to your boss.

2 Complete the sentences with *should* or *shouldn't* and the verbs in the box.

> pay   let   feel   give up   ask
> visit   apologize   do

1 I couldn't believe how rude Paul was. You _____ him speak to you like that!
2 I can't afford to pay my rent. What do you think I _____?
3 We didn't do anything wrong, so we _____ guilty.
4 It wasn't your fault, so I don't think you _____.
5 Boris broke the chair, so I think he _____ for a new one.
6 Your piano classes are going well. You definitely _____!
7 My friend Beatriz is in the hospital. I _____ her later.
8 Do you think Ryan _____ Helen to go out with him?

VOCABULARY: Health and medicine

3 Choose the correct options to complete the sentences.

1 He had to carry a heavy box and now he has a ____.
   a flu   b backache   c sore throat
2 I can't play tennis for weeks because my arm is ____.
   a stressed   b sore   c broken
3 Feel Mila's face to see if she has ____.
   a a temperature b a cold   c an earache
4 I have a painful ____, so I can only eat soup!
   a headache   b earache   c sore throat
5 Felipe has a bad ____; we could hear it during the night.
   a headache   b cough   c toothache
6 Charlie is ____ because he has too much work to do.
   a stressed   b sore   c broken

4 Complete the words. The first letters are given.

1 I touched the hot oven and b_____ my hand.
2 I have a t_____ so I'm going to see the dentist.
3 Don't play with that knife, Henry, or you'll c_____ yourself!
4 Daniel's daughter ate too much ice cream and got a sto_____.
5 The ball hit Luisa in the face and gave her a noseb_____.
6 He h_____ his leg badly and couldn't walk for days.

PRONUNCIATION: should/shouldn't

5  5.1 Listen to the sentences and write *should* or *shouldn't*. Listen, check, and repeat.

1 Do you think I _____ tell Rob the news?
2 Gloria _____ spend so much money on clothes.
3 You _____ talk during class.
4 I agree that David _____ get a new job.
5 Maybe Maria _____ spend more time studying.
6 You really _____ eat so much before exercising!
7 I don't think you _____ worry about that.
8 He _____ put less sugar in his coffee.

SKILLS 5B

LISTENING: Listening in detail

1 ▶ 5.2 Listen to Rebecca calling Joey on the phone. Are the sentences true (T) or false (F)?

1 Joey is Rebecca's brother. ____
2 Joey is at work. ____
3 Joey wasn't feeling well in June. ____
4 Rebecca tells Joey to see a doctor. ____
5 Joey doesn't have a job at the moment. ____
6 Rebecca wants to see Joey. ____

2 ▶ 5.2 Listen again. Choose the best options to complete the sentences.

1 Rebecca thinks Joey is
  a at the doctor's.
  b in bed.
  c with his mother.
2 Rebecca's mother said that Joey had
  a a cough.
  b a sore throat.
  c a cough and a sore throat.
3 In Dallas, Rebecca tried to persuade Joey to
  a see a doctor.
  b get a different job.
  c work fewer hours.
4 Rebecca has a
  a cold.
  b cough.
  c sore throat.
5 Rebecca talks about
  a visiting Joey.
  b cooking a meal for Joey.
  c taking Joey to the doctor's.

3 ▶ 5.3 Read these sentences from Rebecca's phone call. Mark the links between consonant sounds and vowel sounds. Listen and check.

1 I suppose you're in bed taking a nap.
2 ... you're not feeling very well again.
3 She said you had a bad cough and a sore throat.
4 I'm just a little worried about your health.
5 You seemed a little stressed about work when we got together in Dallas.
6 I don't think that job is good for you.

4 Choose the correct verb collocations.

1 When do you usually *make / do / take* your homework?
2 *Make / Have / Take* a deep breath and try to relax.
3 If you *make / do / have* a mistake, draw a line through it.
4 When we *make / have / do* an argument, Sophie always wins!
5 It's a difficult exam, so just *make / do / take* your best.
6 We have to *make / do / have* a decision about where to go on vacation.
7 If you're tired, why don't you *take / make / do* a little nap?
8 Let's *make / take / have* a good talk over coffee.

27

5C LANGUAGE

GRAMMAR: First conditional

1 Order the words to make first conditional sentences. Add commas where necessary.

1 the party / if / have / rains we'll / inside / it
   _____.

2 miss / the / you don't / hurry / bus if / you'll
   _____.

3 Luis I / can give / if I / the message / him / see
   _____.

4 have / problems just / if you / any / call me
   _____.

5 the movies / tired I / if / might not / I'm / go to
   _____.

6 be disappointed / if he / get the / there / job he'll / doesn't
   _____.

7 I have / from / call you / the airport if / enough time / I'll
   _____.

8 if Ellen / her I'll / be home / soon / I'll / calls tell
   _____.

2 Complete the first conditional sentences with the verbs in parentheses in the correct form.

1 If Mike _____ (agree), we _____ (go) on the subway.

2 We _____ (not have) a picnic if the weather _____ (not be) good.

3 Mom _____ (be) angry if we _____ (get) home late.

4 If you _____ (not take) any medicine, you _____ (not feel) better.

5 If the machine _____ (stop), _____ (press) this button.

6 I _____ (call) you if I _____ (need) a ride home.

7 Leonardo _____ (be) upset if we _____ (forget) his birthday.

8 You _____ (hurt) yourself if you _____ (not be) careful!

VOCABULARY: Emotions and feelings

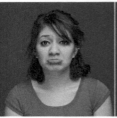

3 Match definitions 1–6 with adjectives a–f.

1 feeling worried about something ____
2 unhappy or sad ____
3 extremely happy about something ____
4 not worried or anxious ____
5 sad because you're alone ____
6 sure of your own abilities ____

a delighted
b confident
c calm
d nervous
e upset
f lonely

4 Complete the adjectives.

1 Her husband was very j_____ and didn't like her talking to other men.

2 Victor was p_____ of his new sneakers and showed them to all his friends.

3 You're very c_____ this morning! What's making you smile so much?

4 When I realized how badly I'd upset her, I felt g_____.

5 She was crying all the time and was extremely m_____.

6 I'm e_____ of your beautiful coat! I wish I had one.

PRONUNCIATION: 'll contraction

5 ▶5.4 Listen to the sentences. Is *will* contracted? Circle the correct answer.

1 contracted / not contracted
2 contracted / not contracted
3 contracted / not contracted
4 contracted / not contracted
5 contracted / not contracted
6 contracted / not contracted
7 contracted / not contracted

SKILLS 5D

WRITING: Writing an informal e-mail

1. Read Izzie's e-mail asking for advice about making friends. Number a–i in the order they appear. The first answer is given.

   a asking about the person you are writing to ___
   b mentioning a completely different subject ___
   c the ending ___
   d the reason for writing ___
   e the greeting ___
   f making an arrangement ___
   g the request for a response ___
   h the subject of the email _1_
   i the details of the problem ___

To: annabrown67@quickmail.com
RE: Advice, please!

Hi Anna!

How's it going? Hope you're enjoying your new job! Did I tell you I left home last month? I'm living in an amazing apartment in Antofagasta now.

That's why I'm writing. I'm having a really bad time, and I wanted to ask you for some advice.

My new apartment's big, and it's nice, but I'm very lonely! I'm a little shy (as you know!), so I'm finding it hard to make new friends. I miss my family so much now that I don't see them very often, especially my mom (I know, I'm such a baby!).

What do you think I should do? How did you make friends when you left home? And when will I stop feeling so bad?!

Anyway, the good news is that my brother's getting married in June! I'm really looking forward to the wedding.

Do you feel like going out for a pizza the next time I'm home, if you aren't too busy? There's a new pizza restaurant. It's kind of expensive, but not too bad. Let me know!

See you later,

Izzie, x

2. Write the contracted forms of these verbs. Which six are in Izzie's e-mail?

   1 you are _____
   2 she has _____
   3 I am _____
   4 it is _____
   5 they have _____
   6 do not _____
   7 there is _____
   8 did not _____
   9 are not _____

3. Complete the sentences with *extremely*, *not very*, *very*, or *a little*. Use each one once.

   1 I want to get more exercise but I'm a _____ nervous about going to a gym.
   2 It's _____ healthy to eat so much junk food.
   3 My friend goes running every day, so she's in _____ good shape.
   4 These dance classes are _____ easy. Anyone can take them.

4. Read the problem below, then write an e-mail to a friend, asking for their advice.

   > *Your doctor says you are very unhealthy.*
   >
   > *You need to get in shape and improve your diet, but you don't know how to.*
   >
   > *You don't play any sports and you love pizza and ice cream.*

   - Structure the e-mail with a subject, greeting, reason for writing, details, request for response and an ending.
   - Use contractions like *I'm* and *don't*.
   - Use informal words like *Hi*, *How's it going?* and *anyway*.
   - Use modifiers like *extremely* and *a little* to make adjectives and adverbs stronger or weaker.

29

5 REVIEW and PRACTICE

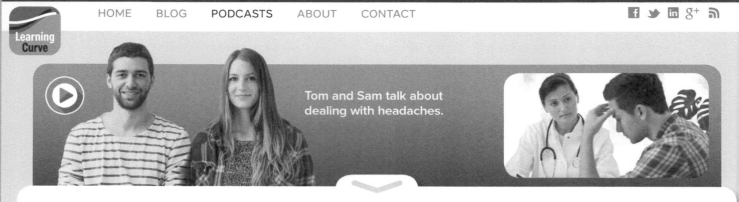

LISTENING

1 ▶ 5.5 Listen to the podcast. Does the speaker say these things? (Circle) *Yes* or *No*.

1	Headaches are the most common health problem in the U.S.	Yes	No
2	Tension headaches are ones that most people get occasionally.	Yes	No
3	Many headaches are caused by people's lifestyles.	Yes	No
4	Sleeping too much can cause headaches.	Yes	No
5	Yoga may help to prevent headaches.	Yes	No

2 ▶ 5.5 Listen again. Complete the sentences with a maximum of three words.

1 In the U.S., more than _____ people have headaches regularly.
2 Bad headaches can make work or functioning in your _____ life difficult.
3 You should see a doctor if you have other symptoms such as a high _____.
4 Tension headaches last for about _____.
5 You can treat most headaches with _____ from the pharmacy.
6 The doctor advises drinking _____ glasses of water daily.
7 It's a good idea to sleep _____ hours every night.
8 Too much work or studying can cause _____, which leads to headaches.

READING

1 Read the blog about how to live to be 100. Match headings A–D with paragraphs 1–4.

A A difficult choice _____
B Don't forget to brush your teeth! _____
C Look at the data _____
D Healthy mind, healthy body _____

2 Choose the correct options to complete the sentences.

1 *Most / Few / Hardly any* people born after 2000 will live to 100.
2 From 1900–2000 life expectancy increased *more than / less than / the same amount as* in previous centuries.
3 People born before 2000 *can / can't / are likely to* live to be 100.
4 *All / Some / None* of the men who took part in the Swedish study were slim and active.
5 To live a long life, it's important to *take medicine / have children / enjoy yourself*.
6 If your father lives to 100, you are *more likely / less likely / about as likely* to live to 100 yourself.
7 For a long life, it *is better / is worse / makes no difference* if you have a young mother.
8 A woman who has a child after 44 has *more chance / less chance / about the same chance* of dying young compared to a woman who has children when she's younger.
9 To live to 100, what's best for the child is *the same as / different from / more important than* what's best for the mother.
10 People with poor teeth are likely to die *before / later than / at the same time as* people with healthy teeth.

REVIEW and PRACTICE 5

HOME   BLOG   PODCASTS   ABOUT   CONTACT

Guest blogger Taylor explains how to live longer.

How to get to 100 ... *and beyond!*

The great news for anyone born after the year 2000 is that they're likely to live to be 100. In fact, life expectancy went up by 30 years between 1900 and 2000—the fastest increase ever! But people born before 2000 shouldn't be too jealous since many scientists say it's possible for them to live longer, too. But health advice seems to change from year to year, so how do we know what we should do if we want to live to 100?

1. Scientists in Sweden followed the lives of 855 men, all born before 1931. Ten of them lived to 100, and they all had certain things in common: they were slim and active, they exercised, they didn't smoke, and they kept themselves busy and cheerful.

2. It seems that if we want to live a long life, we should make sure we have a good time! Research shows that having interests and a feeling of purpose in life often does more to keep us young than pills and medicines. And numerous studies have proven how important it is to have a circle of friends, so you definitely shouldn't spend too much time by yourself.

3. The Swedish study showed that men, whose moms lived into their 80s or 90s, were much more likely to live to an old age themselves. But interestingly, the age of their dads had little effect. Scientists from the University of Chicago found that having a young mom increases your chances of a long life because her eggs were still strong and healthy when she had you. On the other hand, getting pregnant naturally over the age of 44 is a good sign for a woman. According to research from the University of Utah, if you do that, you'll be significantly less likely to die young than a woman who has children at a younger age. If you're a woman, that's a tough decision to make!

4. That's what your parents always told you when you were a child, and it turns out to be very good advice! Scientists have discovered that the bacteria that grow in a dirty mouth can cause heart problems, which may even lead to early death. So, strange as it may seem, if you brush carefully, you can prevent heart attacks as well as a toothache!

UNIT 6 Risks and experiences

6A LANGUAGE

GRAMMAR: Present perfect with *ever* and *never*

1 Choose the correct options to complete the conversation.

> **Gabriela** ¹*Have / Did* you ever been skiing, Juliana?
> **Juliana** No, I ²*didn't / haven't*, but I'd like to. How about you?
> **Gabriela** Yes, I ³*have been / went* once when I was in high school. I loved it.
> **Juliana** Actually, my brother just ⁴*gone / left* for Vail on a skiing trip. He'll be there until Saturday.
> **Gabriela** Lucky him! ⁵*Have / Has* he ever been there before?
> **Juliana** Yes, he's ⁶*went / been* there a few times, although this time he went with his girlfriend, and she's ⁷*never / ever* tried skiing before.

2 Complete the conversations. Write one or two words in each space.

1. **A** _____ you _____ seen a tiger in the wild?
   B Yes, I _____ one in India last year; it was amazing!
2. **A** Have you _____ been to New York?
   B Yes, I _____ there several times.
3. **A** Have you ever tried snowboarding?
   B No, I have _____ done that.
4. **A** _____ Matt ever _____ to Turkey?
   B Yes, he went there last summer.
5. **A** Has your sister ever been engaged?
   B No, she _____.

VOCABULARY: Phrasal verbs

3 Match the two parts of the sentences.

1. Poor Belinda! Her car broke ___
2. I really want to find ___
3. He wants to get in shape and has decided to take up ___
4. Could you buy some coffee? We've run ___
5. It's very hot in here. Could you turn ___
6. I didn't know the word, so I looked it ___

   a out who took my phone.
   b on the air-conditioning, please?
   c up in the dictionary.
   d out of it.
   e riding his bike in the evenings.
   f down on the way to work.

4 Complete the phrasal verbs.

1. I'll borrow your jacket and **give** it _____ on Saturday.
2. Should I **go** _____ writing my essay or finish it later?
3. There should be plenty of gasoline; I **filled** _____ the tank yesterday.
4. It started as a small project, but **turned** _____ a huge job.
5. Could you help me **clean** _____, please?
6. You need to **fill** _____ this application form.
7. I'll be ready in a minute if you just **hold** _____.
8. Felipe has **given** _____ eating meat because of environmental reasons.
9. Shall we keep these magazines or **throw** them _____?
10. I had to **take care** _____ my younger brother while my parents were gone.

PRONUNCIATION: Irregular past participles

5 ▶ 6.1 Practice saying the sentences. Pay attention to the pronunciation of *-en*. Listen, check, and repeat.

1. I've never driv**en** in the snow.
2. Have you ever writt**en** a poem?
3. She's never giv**en** a speech before.
4. Has he ever spok**en** to her?
5. I've never forgott**en** my parents' birthdays.
6. We have never eat**en** at that café.
7. Have you chos**en** your dessert yet?
8. Has she tak**en** her driving test?

32

SKILLS 6B

READING: Guessing the meaning of words from the context

VOLCANO BOARDING
COOL OR CRAZY?

The idea of speeding down the side of a volcano, while **clinging** with all your strength to a little piece of wood, might strike most of us as **terrifying**. But some people travel thousands of miles to do just that. Every year, huge groups of **thrill-seekers** travel to western Nicaragua's Cerro Negro mountain to take part in the new extreme sport of volcano boarding.

Participants, dressed from head to foot in protective clothing, reach speeds of 80 km. per hour on their specially adapted surfboards. They hike up one side of the volcano, take a training class, and then "surf" down the other side, after having paused to admire the **spectacular** view from the top. Some stand as they race down, surfer-style, while others sit. All agree that it's **exhilarating**, though not everyone who does it is in a hurry to repeat it.

"I've never experienced anything like it!" says Jamie White from London. "It's completely **unique**. But although it's great to be able to say I've done it, I'm in no rush to do it again! To **steer**, you hold onto a rope that's attached to the front of the board and pull it one way or the other, but I'm not sure I did it right because I ended up crashing into some rocks. You can slow yourself down by keeping your feet in contact with the ground as you go. But again, I didn't quite **get the hang of** it, and I reached a really scary speed on the way down!"

1 Read the article about a new sport. Are the sentences true (T), false (F), or isn't there enough information to decide (N)?

1. Nicaragua's Cerro Negro mountain is the only place to do this sport. _____
2. You can use an ordinary surfboard for this activity. _____
3. Volcano boarders have to walk up one side of the mountain. _____
4. Jamie White is anxious to take part in this sport again. _____
5. He hurt himself on the way down. _____
6. He was scared by how fast he moved. _____

2 Find the words in **bold** in the text, then choose the correct definitions.

1. If someone is **clinging** to something, they are
   a lying on it.
   b sliding off it.
   c holding it tightly.
2. Something that is **terrifying** is extremely
   a scary.
   b exciting.
   c strange.
3. A **thrill-seeker** is someone who likes
   a doing exciting and dangerous activities.
   b getting a lot of exercise.
   c traveling to new places.
4. A **participant** is someone who
   a has not done something before.
   b trains people to do something.
   c takes part in something.
5. If something is **spectacular**, it is
   a amazing to look at.
   b extremely dangerous.
   c very unusual.
6. An activity that is **exhilarating** makes you feel
   a stressed and worried.
   b happy and excited.
   c relaxed.
7. Something that is **unique** is
   a different from anything else.
   b exactly like something else.
   c very ordinary.
8. To **steer** something is to
   a make it go faster.
   b make it go slower.
   c control its direction.
9. If you **get the hang of** something, you
   a learn how to do it.
   b fail to do it well.
   c start to learn how to do it.

3 Complete the sentences about volcano boarding with the linkers *and*, *also*, *as well*, and *too*.

1. He found volcano boarding very frightening and he _____ found it difficult.
2. Participants experience the thrill of speed and get to see fantastic views, _____.
3. The mountain side is very steep _____ it's also extremely long.
4. People who take part wear special suits. They wear helmets _____.
5. The side of the volcano is hot. It's very hard _____.
6. It's a demanding sport _____ it also requires a degree of training.

33

6C LANGUAGE

GRAMMAR: Second conditional

1 Choose the correct options to complete the sentences.

1 If you could live anywhere in the world, ____?
  a where would you live
  b where do you live
  c where will you live

2 You'd be less tired ____.
  a if you are going to bed earlier
  b if you went to bed earlier
  c if you go to bed earlier

3 If you spoke to Luis, ____.
  a you can explain the situation
  b you could explain the situation
  c you will be able to explain the situation

4 You would lose weight ____.
  a if you ate less
  b if you were eating less
  c if you eat less

5 If you had more money, ____?
  a what did you buy
  b what would you buy
  c what are you buying

6 If you left now, ____.
  a you could take the bus
  b you can take the bus
  c you will be able to take the bus

7 I would take the job ____.
  a if they offer it to me
  b if they are offering it to me
  c if they offered it to me

2 Complete the second conditional sentences with the verbs in parentheses in the correct order.

1 If Manuel ____ to save enough money, he ____ a new motorcycle. (buy, manage)
2 If I ____ you, I ____ Henry for advice. (be, ask)
3 If she ____ more time, she ____ a foreign language. (have, study)
4 Amanda ____ better grades if she ____ harder. (study, get)
5 If you ____ closer to me, we ____ each other more. (live, see)
6 If I ____ rich, I ____ my job. (give up, become)

VOCABULARY: The natural world

3 Order the letters to make words that match the definitions.

1 a small river MASTER ____
2 animals and plants in their natural environment LIDWEFIL ____
3 the land along the edge of the ocean HERSO ____
4 when it gets light in the morning SIRENUS ____
5 a low area of land, often with a river through it LAYVEL ____
6 a huge area of water, like the Atlantic NOACE ____

4 Complete the words. The first letters are given.

1 Those w___ ___ ___ ___ are huge; they'd be great for surfing.
2 There are some fantastic underground c___ ___ ___ ___ that you can explore.
3 The r___ ___ ___ ___ of these trees go several meters deep.
4 There was a fantastic s___ ___ ___ ___ ___ this evening; the sky was pink and orange.
5 I picked some apples from the tree's lower b___ ___ ___ ___ ___ ___ ___.
6 From his room he could see the mountain's snow-covered p___ ___ ___ s.

PRONUNCIATION: Sentence stress

5 ▶ 6.2 Underline the words you think will be stressed. Listen, check, and repeat.

1 If I were you, I'd be annoyed.
2 She'd go back to college if she could afford it.
3 If you could play any instrument, what would it be?
4 If she was taller, she could be a model.
5 If Larissa came to the party, Alex would be happy.
6 I'd join you at the restaurant if I could leave work earlier.
7 Fatima would be happier if she had more friends.
8 If I didn't have to work, I'd go to the movies.

Skills 6D

SPEAKING: Agreeing and disagreeing

1 ▶ 6.3 Listen to Antonio and Carrie discussing vacation plans. Are the statements true (T) or false (F)?

1 Carrie likes Antonio's suggestions for what to do on vacation. _____
2 Antonio wants to do lots of different activities. _____
3 Antonio likes places that are popular with tourists. _____
4 They decide not to go on vacation together. _____

2 ▶ 6.3 Listen again. Match phrases 1–8 with Antonio or Carrie's reasons for using them a–h.

1 Absolutely! _____
2 I don't know. _____
3 Exactly! _____
4 Oh, come on! _____
5 I don't think so. _____
6 I suppose so. _____
7 I'm not sure about that. _____
8 You're right. _____

a Carrie doesn't want fresh air and exercise.
b Antonio admits that they are both tourists.
c Carrie agrees that they should decide on a vacation.
d Antonio agrees with Carrie's suggestion for a vacation.
e Carrie disagrees that being alone would be good.
f Carrie isn't crazy about going on a physically active vacation.
g Antonio prefers not to have Wi-Fi or comfortable beds.
h Antonio doesn't want to stay in a comfortable hotel.

3 ▶ 6.4 Complete the phrases for taking turns. Listen again and check.

1 I want to do something exciting, something that's a physical challenge. What _____?
2 Sorry, Antonio, you _____ ...
3 It would be nice to get away from the rest of the world, _____ think so?
4 Go _____, Carrie.

4 ▶ 6.5 Read the opinions. Then listen and respond using the phrases from exercise 2 and your own reasons.

1 It's best to go on vacation by yourself because you're more likely to meet interesting people.
2 Everyone should travel as much as possible. You can't understand the world if you haven't seen it!
3 Sports like sailing and mountain climbing aren't dangerous if you use the right equipment.
4 All students should take a year off from studying to go traveling.

6 REVIEW and PRACTICE

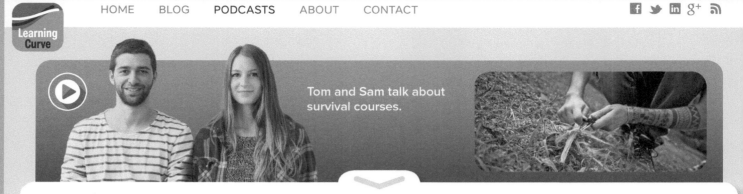

LISTENING

1 🔊 6.6 Listen to the podcast. Number these things 1–5 in the order the speaker mentions them.

a how to find drinking water _____
b figuring out where you are _____
c the kind of people who take survival courses _____
d how to create smoke signals _____
e how to make a fire _____

2 🔊 6.6 Listen again. Choose the correct options to complete the sentences.

1 Sofia's course taught people how to
   a become a soldier.
   b survive in the wild.
   c deal with danger in Canada.
2 Sofia took the course because she
   a knew someone whose plane had crashed.
   b wanted to meet people with different jobs.
   c wanted to learn skills for dangerous situations.
3 The most important thing Sofia learned was how to
   a get water to drink.
   b find food in the wild.
   c make a shelter.
4 Sofia doesn't want to hunt animals because
   a it's too difficult.
   b she doesn't eat meat.
   c they frighten her.
5 Sofia learned how to use the sun to
   a walk in a straight line.
   b cross rivers safely.
   c see where she was walking.
6 Sofia learned how to get help by
   a being prepared.
   b waving to people.
   c lighting a fire.

READING

1 Read the blog about traveling alone. Check (✓) the things the writer talks about.

a safety advice for women _____
b the laws in different countries _____
c choosing the best restaurants _____
d finding the cheapest flights _____
e organizing accommodations _____
f meeting the local people _____

2 Are the statements true (T) or false (F), according to the blog?

1 Other travelers can often give you useful tips. _____
2 The writer had an enjoyable vacation traveling around Turkey. _____
3 When traveling with friends, you sometimes have to do things you don't enjoy. _____
4 It's good to be able to change your mind about what you want to do on a vacation. _____
5 Women are always in more danger than men when traveling alone. _____
6 Drinks are usually more expensive in other countries. _____
7 It's sometimes better to find out about a country when you arrive, not before. _____
8 People who try traveling by themselves may find they prefer it. _____

REVIEW and PRACTICE 6

HOME　　BLOG　　PODCASTS　　ABOUT　　CONTACT

Guest blogger Ethan gives some tips on traveling by yourself.

Vacationing alone

Have you ever taken a vacation alone? For many people, it's a terrifying thought. They worry about being lonely, that accommodations will cost more, and that it might be dangerous. But it doesn't have to be that way!

If you go with a friend, you'll probably spend the whole time talking to him/her, but if you go by yourself, you're more likely to meet local people. Some of my most sociable trips have been to places without many tourists. Talk to taxi drivers, waiters, store owners; you'll get a lot of advice you can't find in the guidebooks! On the whole, people are remarkably friendly and generous. One of the best trips I've ever taken was to a remote area of Turkey, where several people invited me for meals in their own homes.

And just imagine, no more boring art galleries when you'd rather be white-water rafting, instead. And no more hanging around stores while your friend tries on fifteen different hats. Or if you just feel like spending the day under a tree with a book, there's nobody to complain!

It's worth giving yourself the flexibility to change your mind. If you plan everything before you go, you can end up missing out on unexpected opportunities. You might get an invitation to somewhere wonderful, or you might decide you love a place and don't want to move on. But if you know you're going to arrive somewhere late in the evening, make sure you reserve a hotel in advance. You don't want to be wandering around strange streets at night with nowhere to go.

And what about women travelers? Well, they can and do have equally good experiences as men. That doesn't mean there aren't some risks. Obviously you shouldn't get in a car with someone you just met, for example, but that's just common sense, isn't it? It's worth putting the number for the police on your phone. And be careful in cafés and bars to make sure nobody puts anything in your drink. Some unlucky travelers have woken up several hours later with no money or passport.

Finally, do your research before you go. Find out about the local culture and social attitudes. How should you dress to avoid negative attention? Are there any typical tricks that thieves use on tourists?

So should we all be brave and try it? I definitely think so. The only danger I can see is that you may never want to go on vacation with your friends or family again!

WRITING PRACTICE

WRITING: Making notes

1 Read Anup's blog about the best year of his life. Then complete it with reasons and results a–f.

a it had been snowing heavily
b I started talking to a young woman on the platform
c I was able to travel and see the world
d it reminds me of that wonderful year
e I really wanted to go there
f it was so interesting

This photograph shows me in front of the Taj Mahal in India. The year was 2012, and it was the best year of my life!

I finished college that summer, but my new job didn't start until the end of the year. That's why ¹_____.
I spent a lot of that time in India, and it was absolutely amazing! I went to England as a young child, but I was born in India, so ²_____. I even brought back some photos of the house where I'd lived with my parents.

In November of that year, I finally started my career as a journalist. It was hard work, but that's why ³_____. I was lucky to have a fantastic boss who taught me a lot, and it was great to have a job that I knew I was going to love.

And finally, the best thing of all that happened in 2012, was that one day my train was two hours late because ⁴_____. I was bored and fed up, so ⁵_____. Did I fall in love that day? Well, maybe not that day, but I did like her enough to invite her to dinner, and we got married two years later.

Life is still great, but if I need to cheer myself up for any reason, I get this photo out and look at it because ⁶_____.

2 Think about the best year of your life. Write notes about it on the mind map. You can invent ideas—they don't have to be true! You can leave some clouds empty or add new clouds.

3 Read the sentences. Do they talk about reasons or results?

1 2014 was the best year of my life because I got my driver's license that year.	reason	result
2 I wanted to be a doctor, so I had to work hard in school.	reason	result
3 I went swimming every day. That's why I was in such good shape.	reason	result
4 My boss was out of town, so I had the chance to do her job.	reason	result
5 I was really pleased because I passed all my exams.	reason	result

4 Write three sentences like the ones in exercise 3. Use *because*, *so*, and *That's why* and ideas from your mind map.

5 Write a blog about the best year of your life.

- Write about at least three good things that happened, using your notes from exercise 2.
- Write as many ideas as you can about these three main topics.
- Choose the best ideas then organize them into three paragraphs.
- Include at least three sentences with *because*, *so*, or *that's why*.

WRITING PRACTICE

WRITING: Writing a narrative

1 Read the story about how Ed got a job. Which paragraph (1–4) is missing?

1 the background   2 a problem   3 a resolution   4 the ending

It was 2014, and I wasn't happy. There I was, 22 years old, with a good degree in computer studies, but I was working as a waiter for a company that didn't treat its employees well. I kept applying for computer jobs, but companies always wanted people with experience working with computers. Without a job, I couldn't get experience, and without experience, I couldn't get a job. The situation seemed impossible.

Then one day, I was working at a party given by a large car company. Before the guests started eating, the boss wanted to give a presentation. He was using notes that were on his computer, but in the middle of his presentation, it suddenly stopped working.

He tried hard to fix the problem, but it still wouldn't work. He started to look nervous. Everyone was waiting for him to finish speaking so they could eat. When I offered to help, he looked surprised, but agreed to let me try. Fortunately, I immediately saw what was wrong and quickly got his computer working again.

2 Complete the sentences with the simple past or past continuous form of the verbs in parentheses.

1 Ed was working as a waiter, but he _____ for a better job at the same time. (look)
2 Ed _____ to be a waiter. (not want)
3 Ed _____ enough experience to get a computer job. (not have)
4 The boss's computer stopped working while he _____. (speak)
5 Ed successfully _____ the computer. (fix)

3 Find words in the story to complete these sentences. Are they adjectives or adverbs?

1 Ed didn't feel _____ in 2014.   adjective   adverb
2 The waiters weren't treated _____.   adjective   adverb
3 The computer _____ stopped working.   adjective   adverb
4 The boss tried _____ to get the the computer to work again.   adjective   adverb
5 He began to look _____.   adjective   adverb
6 Ed repaired the computer _____.   adjective   adverb

4 Use these pictures to write the missing paragraph of the story.

- Try to write five sentences. Describe what happened, how Ed felt, and what the situation is now.
- Use verbs in the simple past and past continuous.
- Use adjectives and adverbs to make your paragraph interesting.

WRITING PRACTICE

WRITING: Writing an informal e-mail asking for advice

1 Read Michael's e-mail asking for advice about a trip. Then number a–i in the order in which they appear in the e-mail (1–9). The first answer is given.

○ ○ ○

To: robknight5@openmail.com

RE: Advice

Hi Rob!

[1]How's it going? Are you still going running every day? [2]I'm going climbing in the Himalayas in the spring, but I'm a little worried about it. That's why I'm writing. I know [3]you've been to Nepal, and I wanted to ask you for some advice.

I really love walking, as you know, but I've never done anything like this. It sounds extremely tough and I'm scared [4]it'll be too difficult for me. I'm not in very good shape right now. What do you think I should do? Can you give me some ideas about how to prepare, and what I should take with me? [5]What's the best way to get in better shape in three months? Can you send me some tips?

Anyway, I guess [6]it's good to try new things. Seb told me you've taken up painting. He says [7]you're pretty good at it!

Do you feel like going for coffee sometime soon? Then I can ask you some more questions about my trip.

See you later,

Michael

a asking about the person you're writing to	____	**f** the request for a response	____
b the ending	____	**g** mentioning a different subject	____
c the greeting	____	**h** the subject	_1_
d making an arrangement	____	**i** the details of the problem	____
e the reason for writing	____		

2 Look at the underlined contractions in the e-mail (1–7) and write the full forms.

3 Complete these phrases from the e-mail with modifiers. Then number them 1–5, from the strongest to the weakest.

1 I'm _____ worried about it. ____

2 I _____ love walking, as you know ... ____

3 It sounds _____ tough ... ____

4 I'm not in _____ good shape right now. ____

5 ... he says you're _____ good at it! ____

4 Read the problem in the box, then write an e-mail to a friend, asking for advice.

> You have decided to take up a sport or activity that involves a risk.
> Your parents think it is too dangerous and they don't want you to do it.
> You want to do it, but you don't want to hurt yourself.

- Structure the e-mail with a subject, greeting, reason for writing, details, request for response, and an ending.
- Use contractions like *I'm* and *don't*.
- Use informal words and phrases like *Hi, How's it going?,* and *anyway*.
- Use modifiers like *extremely* and *a little* to make adjectives and adverbs stronger or weaker.

76

NOTES

NOTES

NOTES

58 St Aldates
Oxford
OX1 1ST
United Kingdom

Second reprint: 2024
ISBN: 978-84-668-2940-3

© Richmond / Santillana Global S.L. 2018

All rights reserved. No part of this book may be reproduced, stored in a retrieval system or transmitted in any form by any means, electronic, mechanical, photocopying, recording or otherwise, without the prior permission in writing of the Publisher.

Publishing Director: Deborah Tricker
Publisher: Simone Foster
Media Publisher: Sue Ashcroft
Workbook Publisher: Luke Baxter
Content Developer: David Cole-Powney
Editors: Debra Emmett, Helen Ward, Ruth Cox, Emma Clarke, Fiona Hunt, Eleanor Clements, Helen Wendholt
Proofreaders: Peter Anderson, Jamie Bowman, Tas Cooper, Fiona Hunt, Amanda Leigh
Design Manager: Lorna Heaslip
Cover Design: This Ain't Rock'n'Roll, London
Design & Layout: Lorna Heaslip, Oliver Hutton, Gabriela Alvarez
Photo Researcher: Magdalena Mayo
Learning Curve video: Mannic Media
Audio production: Eastern Sky Studios
App development: The Distance
Americanization: Diane Hermanson

We would also like to thank the following people for their valuable contribution to writing and developing the material:
Alastair Lane, Bob McLarty, Claire Thacker, Louis Rogers, Rachael Roberts, Pamela Vittorio (Video Script Writer), Belen Fernandez (App Project Manager), Rob Sved (App Content Creator)

Illustrators:
Simon Clare; Dermot Flynn c/o Dutch Uncle; Guillaume Gennet, Julien Kern and Liav Zabari c/o Lemonade; Joanna Kerr c/o New Division; Piers Sandford c/o Meiklejohn; The Boy FitzHammond and Beverley Young, c/o NB Illustration

Photos:
J. Jaime; J. Lucas; 123RF/ lightpoet; ALAMY/IanDagnall Laptop Computing, John Birdsall, Chuck Place, Granger Historical Picture Archve, All Canada Photos, Cofiant Images, ONOKY - Photononstop, Action Plus Sports Images, Arcaid Images, Jasminko Ibrakovic, Image Source Salsa, Radius Images, Pat Behnke, Ann Cutting, 360b, Heritage Image Partnership Ltd, Roger Bamber, Cultura Creative (RF), Blend Images, RosalreneBetancourt 10, Nick Gregory, BSIP SA, Trinity Mirror / Mirrorpix, Wavebreak Media ltd, Torontonian, Joy Sunny, SWNS, TP, IanDagnall Computing, PhotoEdit, Ammentorp Photography, Peter Barritt, Cliff Hide Stock, greenwales, caia image, eye35.pix, Carlos Guerra, Janine Wiedel Photolibrary, Peter Titmuss, Richard Heyes, Motoring Picture Library, Helen Hotson, Cephas Picture Library, ACORN 1, tommaso altamura, Steve Davey Photography, Image Source, Bill Cheyrou, Agencja Fotograficzna Caro, Kreative Photography, Imagedoc, Lou-Foto, Julie g Woodhouse, allesalltag, Stefano Carvoretto, MAX EAREY, wareham.nl (sport), Duncan Snow, Wilawan Khasawong, Brian Overcast, Design Pics Inc, Westend61 GmbH, Anton Stariskov, Elina Manninen, Aflo Co., Ltd., Alan Smith, Classic Image, Photos 12, D. Hurst, MBI, AF archive, PjrTravel, FineArt, moodboard, DonSmith, Jeramey Lende, epa european pressphoto agency b.v.; BNPS (BOURNEMOUTH NEWS & PICTURE SERVICE)/ Rijksmuseum/ BNPS; CATERS NEWS AGENCY/ Caters News Agency; GETTY IMAGES SALES SPAIN/Lumi Images/Dario Secen, Graham Monro/gm photographics, Jetta Productions, Thomas_EyeDesign, Photos.com Plus, David M. Benett, Astrid Stawiarz, Mark Metcalfe, CARL DE SOUZA, Alistair Berg, Toby Burrows, Sam Edwards, Dave Hogan, Barcroft, Maskot, Bloomberg, Bettmann, Don Arnold, Kari Lehr, PETER MACDIARMID, RENE SLAMA, Boston Globe, CHRISTOPHE ARCHAMBAULT, Caiaimage/Paul Bradbury, Image source, Paul Chesley, Thinkstock; HIGHRES PRESS STOCK/AbleStock.com; ISTOCKPHOTO/SeanShot, Pali Rao, oztasbc, jojoo64, SondraP, MollyNZ, Geber86, xijian, vgajic, sturti, olaser, miralex, mergez, alexsl, HASLOO, SolStock, DONOT6, Getty Images Sales Spain, Devasahayam Chandra Dhas, monkeybusinessimages, Osmany Torres Martín, alessandroguerriero, AleksandarGeorgiev, Tommaso Altamura, Nicolas McComber, warrengoldswain, travellinglight, stevecoleimages, Robyn Mackenzie, German-skydiver, digitalskillet, Wavebreakmedia, Petar Chernaev, Jaroslav Frank, wundervisuals, Squaredpixels, LuckyBusiness, Julia Nichols, Drazen Lovric, Dean Mitchell, elenaleonova, PeopleImages, Elenathewise, Dieter Meyrl, Daniel Ernst, Cathy Yeulet, ozgurdonmaz, mediaphotos, Yuri_Arcurs, Visiofutura, Jason Poole, David Sucsy, Bulent Ince, nataistock, bluehill75, calvindexter, MartialRed, Juanmonino, FangXiaNuo, Joel Carillet, FSTOPLIGHT, DeluXe-PiX, DeanDrobot, g-stockstudio, zhudifeng, pixdeluxe, milanfoto, dolgachov, cindygoff, SteveTram, OcusFocus, robertcicchetti, Maxiphoto, Kaan Ates, Huchen Lu, Anna Bryukhanova, Halfpoint, CactuSoup, yipengge, mihailomilovanovic, urbancow, rcaucino, pepifoto, lucky336, kyoshino, denphumi; MAYANG MURNI ADNIN; NASA/ NASA; REX SHUTTERSTOCK/Jonathan Player, ABC Inc/ Everett, Peter Brooker, Kippa Limited, Pixelformula, Newspix; SHUTTERSTOCK; SHUTTERSTOCK NETHERLANDS,B.V.; Project Jacquard/Levi's Strauss; Library of Congress/wikipedia; Carpigiani Gelato University; Niccolo Casas /EMBR labs; Optomen Television Ltd.; courtesy of Alex Deans; Pauline Van Dongen; Alastair Humphreys; freepic.com; Ringly Inc.; Jon Barlow; Dave Homcy; ALAMY/Frances Roberts, Nick Baylis, REUTERS, David Taylor, Paul Nichols, Mode Images, M L Pearson, Jeremey Richards, Panther Media GmbH, Big Cheese Photo LLC, Digital Image Library, Sabena Jane Blackbird, www.BibleLandPictures. com, Purcell Team; GETTY IMAGES SALES SPAIN/ Thinkstock; ISTOCKPHOTO/Getty Images Sales Spain; REX SHUTTERSTOCK/Solent News; ARCHIVO SANTILLANA; Images used under licence from ©Shutterstock.com

Cover Photo: Jon Barlow

We would like to thank the following reviewers for their valuable feedback which has made Personal Best possible. We extend our thanks to the many teachers and students not mentioned here.

Brad Bawtinheimer, Manuel Hidalgo, Paulo Dantas, Diana Bermúdez, Laura Gutiérrez, Hardy Griffin, Angi Conti, Christopher Morabito, Hande Kokce, Jorge Lobato, Leonardo Mercato, Mercilinda Ortiz, Wendy López

The Publisher has made every effort to trace the owner of copyright material; however, the Publisher will correct any involuntary omission at the earliest opportunity

Printed in Brazil by Forma Certa Gráfica Digital
Lote: 800.398